Memoirs of a Diabetic:

A Malaysian

SIVARAJAH MANICAVASAGAR

PARTRIDGE

A Penguin Random House Company

To order additional copies of this book, contact
Toll Free 800 101 2657 (Singapore)
Toll Free 1 800 81 7340 (Malaysia)
orders.singapore@partridgepublishing.com

www.partridgepublishing.com/singapore

CONTENTS

Acknowledgments

I wish to extend my greatest thanks and appreciation to my late parents. My father S. Manicavasagar passed on in 1997, and my mother Annaledchumy Ammal passed on in 1986.

My mother, especially an emotional person by nature, had to endure so much stress taking care of me not only with diabetes but also earlier with the frequent visits to doctors for tonsillitis. Then came the attack of mumps, then jaundice, and later shingles. It should be remembered that most people did not own cars then. The only transport was by bus and tricycles.

Strangely enough, my mother also had diabetes when she was in her late fifties, and she also went on insulin. In fact, she preferred me to inject her with insulin, in spite of the fact that my sister, Dr. Rajeswari, is a doctor. The needles were metal, not the disposable ones we have now.

I also wish to show all the appreciation and heartfelt thanks to my eldest sister, Madam Sarojini Vijayaratnam, and her late husband Supt. Vijayaratnam; my brother-in-law Dr. Asohandran Arasaradnam; and my sister Dr. Rajeswari. I also have to thank both of my brothers and my nephews, nieces, and grandnephews and nieces too. All of them and their spouses have been a great support to me.

It would be truly an insult to my wife if I were negligent in mentioning her. Rajalakshmi has truly been great and caring. It has been thirty-seven years since we were married, and I should say that she is a marvelous person. For all the nonsense I do—I mean, being too careful, resulting in low sugar levels—she has not once showed her irritation or anger and reprimanded me.

I am ever grateful to my spiritual guru who himself is a prolific writer on spiritual matters and in impeccable English. He is Swami Bhoomananda Tirtha of Kerala in India. When I asked him for his blessings, he blessed me and told me to "just write." By that, he meant write for the sake of writing and the joy.

I would herein thank Desiree Bello and Shelly Edmunds, both of Trafford Publishing, especially Miss Edmunds, for taking all the pains to coerce me into getting on with this project.

I would like to show my heartfelt gratitude to Mr Gan Ber Zin, the manager of Newway Pharmacy, Jalan Rasah. He researched and printed copies of pictures of glass syringes and metal needles used in the fifties through seventies. More importantly, Mr. Gan was instrumental in making me apply and subsequently get free supplies of glucosamine sachets and adaxil capsules, which the government bears the costs of. As a retiree from the government service, I'm entitled to these benefits. Had I purchased them on my own, they would have cost me a fortune, bearing in mind that these have to be taken daily. In this respect, I wish to thank the government of Malaysia for its services.

Last, I wish to thank Mr. Lai Sen Nyi of Ban Yin Medical Store for consenting to photograph a spirit lamp that he still uses for medicinal purposes. I searched all over to get one, but he was the one who finally relieved me.

INTRODUCTION

Diabetes mellitus is categorized as type 1 or type 2 diabetes. Type 1 diabetes is also known as juvenile onset diabetes, and once diagnosed, daily doses of insulin have to be administered. Type 2 diabetes, on the other hand, is adult onset diabetes and generally associated with obesity, lack of exercise, and insulin resistance. For type 2, on initial diagnosis, diabetic patients are put on pills. But very often due to lack of care, these very same patients are asked to take daily doses of insulin just like the type 1 diabetics. For type 2 diabetics who were on pills due to apathy as far as food consumption is concerned and/or lack of exercise resulting in high blood sugar level readings, doctors advise that they resort to insulin.

There is a distinct difference between a type 1 diabetic and a type 2 diabetic. From day one, a type 1 diabetic has to resort to daily injections of insulin. The type 1 diabetic was formerly called a juvenile diabetic, as was my case. But now type 1 is the term that is commonly used.

As for type 2 diabetics, from my observations, despite the publicity via the mass media and the electronic media on the dangers and necessary care associated with diabetes, many type 2 diabetics remain careless and carefree, and as a consequence, they are forced to go on daily doses of insulin. Many curse and swear when they are forced to face the prospect of these restrictions and more so of injections of insulin on a day-to-day basis.

Even to this day, many patients, especially in rural areas, are unaware that insulin and pills are not a cure and that, in spite of administering these, neglect should not be had in diet and physical activities. Juvenile diabetics and Type 1 diabetics who then and now are on daily insulin injection administration, sometimes more than once a day have only one choice that is they have to be on insulin injections daily.

In my memoirs, I have given an account of all the major incidents of hypoglycemic (low blood sugar) and hyperglycemic (high blood sugar) attacks as accurately as possible. I have compiled incidents from the year 1957 when I was just eleven years old until 2013, when I'm now a sixty-seven-year-old man, so this covers a span of nearly fifty-six years.

With much regret, I apologize that I do not have all the specific dates of various incidents herein mentioned, but so far as the events are concerned, the years mentioned are correct.

My other regret is that I do not have photographs of the old General Hospital and the wards in which I was admitted. Very few people in the 1950s and 1960s owned cameras. These were very expensive, along with film and its development. I owned my first camera in the mid-1970s.

However, I have taken photographs of the area where the second-class ward and admission room of the old General Hospital were then situated. I was admitted to this second-class ward for the first time in 1957 and once again in 1958. The area has now been cleared and made into a car park.

Readers, especially the youthful ones, should keep in mind that the conditions and situations in the 1950s and even later in Malaysia were very different from what they are today. So they have to be imaginative to relate to what I have written about.

It is my utmost wish that whoever reads this memoir will be able to realize that we are presently very fortunate in having advanced in getting patients the right and proper care of their diabetic conditions and therefore to lead perfectly normal lives, and we are still moving forward. After all, I personally feel that some discipline is necessary to lead a diabetic life in such a way that diabetics do not and should never become a burden to their family members. Diabetics should be masters of their disease, which I am sorry to say that their own excessive indulgence in food and failure to burn off all the excesses has brought about. Of course, in cases of genetic predispositions and heredity, nothing can be said. It is beyond anyone's control.

CHAPTER 1

The Dawning of a Truth

In 1957, I was an eleven-year-old studying in King George V Primary School in Seremban in the state of Negeri Sembilan in Malaysia. I was in primary five. Like all youngsters, I was very active physically, and most evenings, I used to play with children in the neighborhood. In 1957, there were no computers, let alone computer games. There were no mobile phones or even television. So, there were only two important things for school-going children. One was to go to school; the other was to entertain ourselves in the evenings by playing games. We played games like spinning tops, marbles, and football, or we even went round the neighborhood rolling tires or bicycle rims. Roads were safe, as there were very few vehicles. Not many people had land phones. In fact, these land phones could be seen only in the homes of the well-to-do or those in the essential services. Other than the activities mentioned previously, the boys also indulged in flying kites. Life was never boring then, as it is now too. But in this year, 1957, my life and lifestyle changed suddenly.

My father, S. Manicavasagar, was a chief clerk in the land office in Seremban, my hometown. My mother, Annaledchumy Ammal, was a housewife. Sometime in the middle or later part of 1957, I had symptoms of frequent and uncontrollable thirst for no apparent reasons known to us. Being very active and consequently drinking lots of water was understandable, but continuous drinking of water due to thirst in spite of not exercising was strange.

I used to drink lots of water from the taps in school and at home. Tap water then was very safe to drink, and it was clean. I had never seen a water filter then, nor had I even tasted filtered water. Most people did not boil water, even for drinking purposes. If ever they did so, it was for making beverages. Although there was electricity, most of the cooking and boiling was done by using firewood and/or charcoal.

After much drinking, the natural result would be to ease myself, not a few times but very often. This urge to wee was so strong that I used to run out of class as quickly as possible at school without the teacher's permission in order to wee and then run back to class. I once even wet my pants in school. Fortunately, only one of my friends noticed it and told me about the stench of urine. I was very embarrassed. I did not relate any of these things to my parents because I had no inkling about my body's condition or what was to come.

CHAPTER 2

Awareness of Diabetes

In 1957, very few people, especially children in Malaysia were diagnosed with diabetes. Fewer still were the number of adults who had a good comprehension of this disease called diabetes. Those who had some such knowledge did not understand the severity or symptoms of the disease. What they often wrongly understood was that, if a child were ever afflicted with diabetes, his life span was "guaranteed" to be a short one.

Today, so much prominence is given to all the media, especially medical talk shows on television. We had no television then. The media then, both the radio and press, gave little prominence to discussing these health concerns because diabetes was not as prevalent. The Internet these days is also of great help.

Also in 1957, students from both genders were taken on a trip to the historical city of Melaka, about fifty miles away from my hometown. All students had to get the consent of either their parents or guardians in writing. Being still unaware of my diabetic condition, I also decided to go.

As students, we had studied about Melaka and how the Portuguese and Dutch, respectively, had colonized it in the sixteenth and seventeenth centuries, respectively. These two colonial powers had left behind great monuments that still stand, and even today, millions of tourists come to this city.

Structures such as the A Famosa (a fortress), a legacy of the Portuguese, are still marvels to look at. There are also many Dutch monuments that still stand and are attractions for tourists. The Dutch overran the Portuguese garrisons in 1641, about 130 years after the conquest by the Portuguese in 1511.

We had the opportunity to visit the still-preserved grave of the great saint St. Francis Xavier. I enjoyed myself, but I also had to endure uncontrollable thirst and, consequently, frequent urges to answer the call of nature. As a youngster, it was only natural that I indulged in sweet stuffs and ice cream like other students. But unlike other students, I had to endure thirst. To quench this thirst, I drank bottled drinks, and this made matters worse.

For lunch, my fellow students and I were taken to a sort of food court and enjoyed ourselves under the supervision of teachers. It was then time to return home. It was already past seven o'clock, and it was getting dark. On the return journey, I had to endure a very full bladder waiting to burst. Fortunately, another student also wanted to ease himself, so the teacher directed the driver to pull over to the side of the road to enable us to ease ourselves. In 1957, R & R areas were unheard of in my country. Roads were not as brightly lit as they are today. In fact, one could easily count the number of vehicles passing by as the vehicles were very few in number.

About one and a half hours later, we finally reached the designated area where our parents were waiting to pick us up.

As for me, I did not enjoy the trip for the simple reason that I had to handle a dry throat, parched lips, thirst, and an urge to release a constantly full bladder. This was perhaps an indication of what was to come later.

CHAPTER 3

Condition Worsens

My condition turned from bad to worse. Soon I started bed-wetting at night. Often while it was happening, I used to think that I was using the toilet. This bed-wetting became very frequent, and my poor mother had to wash the bedsheets and blanket and even dry the bed in the sun every so often. Washing machines were unheard of in 1957.

This continued, and very soon, my mother suspected what she had been thinking all along when she saw ants favoring the place I had urinated on. As my father was a government employee, he was given a quarters (house). These houses then were built of planks and wood, and they stood on concrete stilts.

As children, we used to wee in the drain nearest to the outer drains and then pour water in the drain to clear and clean it. My mother related this "ant" incident to my father. My father then asked an uncle, Assapillai, to take me to the town clinic to have my urine tested for sugar.

In 1957, even hospitals in Malaysia did not have the test strips and glucometers that are used today. At that time, urine tests measured a person's diabetic condition. The only test then was to collect the urine in a bottle or cup, fill a test tube with about an inch of Benedict or Fehling's solution, add eight drops of urine to this solution, and heat the test tube over a spirit lamp. When the Benedict solution (blue in color) was heated over the flame, it would show the state of the sugar in the urine. I say urine sugar and not blood sugar, as no test for blood sugar was available then.

Mr. Selvarajah (now passed on) did the urine sugar test at the town clinic, and he was also the father of my very close friend and classmate C. S. Soman (now a retired colonel). After testing the blood sugar, Mr. Selvarajah was shocked and showed the test tube to my uncle. I saw it too. The color was brick red, the last and worst reading for a urine sugar test.

The Benedict or Fehling's solution is blue in color. After adding the eight drops of urine to the solution and heating the test tube over the spirit lamp, if the color still remains blue, it is termed "NiL"—in other words, normal. If the color changes to a very light green, it is called "trace." If the color is slightly darker than trace (green), then it is called one plus (+). If the color changes to even a darker green, it is known as two plus (++). When the color changes to yellow, it is called three plus (+++). This is not a good reading. The next reading that is considered very bad is the color orange, or four plus (++++). The last and worst of all the readings is the brick-red color, the reading of my urine sample when it was tested.

We now know that these tests are inaccurate, but in 1957 and even years later, this was the test.

CHAPTER 4

Totally Unaffected

I was in the dark about what this excitement was about. I couldn't comprehend a thing about the test and how and why it would affect me. I did know that I had uncontrollable thirst, frequent urination, and bed-wetting. I had not even known what the word "diabetes" was until after my urine sample was tested. In the Tamil language, my mother tongue, it is known as *inipu neer*, sweet liquid.

After the test, with a concerned and sad face, my uncle took me back home to relate the news to my mother and later my father. My parents were shocked, and my mother, an emotional person by nature, cried a lot. But I was totally unfazed. However, in hindsight, I now say that my parents should not have been unduly affected, as all the symptoms were already there. Perhaps knowledge on diabetes was not prevalent then. Maybe my parents, especially my mother, in spite of seeing all the diabetic symptoms, were hoping that this would not be the case with me.

I think my mom was the most affected by the diagnosis, as prior to this she had had to contend with a very bad case of tonsillitis that I had. As a young boy, like my contemporaries, I liked to play games in the hot sun, and this aggravated the tonsillitis. Every time this happened, my mother used to take me to a private clinic for Dr. Samuel to treat me. This clinic, now renovated, still exists but is being run by his son presently. For tonsillitis, I was injected with intramuscular penicillin injections. Those needles were long and often painful. Later, I was treated with oral antibiotics until the tonsils were removed in 1973.

Fig. 1. Picture of Samuel Clinic as renovated.

CHAPTER 5

Further Tests and Consultation

Following my blood test, my father, with the help of my uncle, Mr. Assapillai, took me to the town clinic the next day for further examination by doctors, who subjected me to further testing. The other test that was done was a test known as a ketone or acetone test to see if the patient had a possibility of going into a hyperglycemic state (high blood sugar).

Fig. 2. Town clinic then , now renovated and
named District Health Office.

After the test, I was immediately asked to be admitted to the General Hospital. Prior to being admitted, the state physician, a South African Chinese man, Dr. Francis Wong Lun King, examined me. My father was present during this examination.

I was admitted to the second-class ward. I was put in a single room with doors that could revolve. Not many single rooms were on the upper level. On the lower level of the second-class ward, there were multiple beds arranged in two rows.

Fig. 3. Second-class ward then, now car park.
1) Single bedded rooms with revolving doors and
2) multi-bedded ward (also see page 110).

Now this place has been demolished to make way for a car park. On the day I was admitted, my mother brought along my clothes. She told a very kind and gentle attendant, Markandan, who she and my father knew, to place a Mackintosh sheet beneath the bedsheet in the event I urinated on the bed at night after I had slept. Sure enough, this did take place a few times. The bedsheets had to be changed. But if not for the Mackintosh sheet, the bed would have been wet too.

I was in the ward for about two or three weeks, mainly to be stabilized on insulin. This was the first time I came to know a sentence had been passed on me. I had to be on insulin for the rest of my life, and that meant daily doses of injections too. I was subjected to urine sugar tests every four hours or so, and if the level showed high sugar content, then I was injected with a small dose of soluble (fast-acting) insulin. Even at midnight, the nurses used to awaken me to take my body temperature and to collect the urine for tests to be done.

After a few days or a week of testing and retesting and adjustments to the dosage of soluble insulin, the doctors were finally able to essentially prescribe the insulin dosage I had to be given. After I had been admitted, my mother asked me if I wanted her to stay with me at the hospital. But I refused. I knew the trauma she had already undergone, and though young, I did not want to trouble her or anyone else. However, she told Mr. Markandan to keep an eye on me. This attendant was a gem. He spoke very kindly to me, perhaps because of my age, and sometimes late at night, he would come and check on me while I was sleeping.

CHAPTER 6

A Life Sentence of Daily Insulin Injections

I cannot remember precisely the dosage of insulin that was prescribed, but I know it was not low. For a child diagnosed with diabetes, there arises a problem, which medical officers told to my father. First, as a diabetic food consumption had to be well regulated. On the other hand, a growing child needs good nourishment and good intake of food. So, this was a contradiction of sorts. This is true because I too faced the same problem until early adulthood. The nurses started injecting me with protamine zinc insulin (PZI), a long-acting insulin. At the ward, the doctors kept readjusting the dosage until I was stabilized. Dr. Francis Wong didn't come very often because of his busy schedule, being the state physician. At that time, there was only one physician in the hospital and the state. We have come a long way since 1957. Now there are so many physicians.

After about three weeks of stay at the ward, I was finally discharged. Being discharged was one matter, but who was to take me to the hospital for daily injections? The injections had to be administered in the mornings. My father did not have a car. The hospital was about three miles away from my house. I had to go to school in the mornings. So this was a dilemma for my parents.

Finally, my uncle, the taxi driver, agreed to pick me up early in the mornings. My mother used to awaken me at five in the morning, and then I would get into the car.

Five in the morning was really dark and quiet. Streetlights were not the fluorescent type; consequently, streets were not brightly lit. Although getting up at five seemed a burden, on the brighter side of it, I quite enjoyed it because, as my uncle was a taxi driver, he would be going around the town looking for passengers. For me, it was also sightseeing.

At about six, I was sent to the admission room at the old General Hospital to be injected with insulin. Once when my uncle sent me too early, at about five thirty, the hospital assistant was grumpy, ticked at my uncle for bringing me so early.

Fig. 4. (Frontal view of Admission room, now renovated and converted into Drive Thru pharmacy.)

In a way, the hospital assistant was right because, when I was in school, if my insulin was injected too early in the morning, I used to perspire and lose concentration in class late in the day. This was a clear symptom of a hypoglycemic (low blood sugar) attack. This situation would continue until I reached home.

Keeping hormonal changes balanced in a young lad with a necessary intake of food and nutrients for growth was necessary, but at the same time, maintaining good sugar level control as a diabetic was very important in my case too. Most days in school, at about eleven or so, symptoms of hypoglycemia would surface. I would usually be perspire and get dreamy, not concentrating on lessons being taught. This would continue until school was dismissed at about one. Mentally, I was in another world, though I was in class physically. I would feel sleepy and just keep yawning continuously. Concentration in lessons in the later part of the day was a zero. These symptoms continued until I completed my secondary school education in 1963. Luckily, in all my years as a student, not once was I affected by an insulin coma, that is hypoglycemia.

One may wonder why people in my family and I didn't do anything about this. The short and simple reason is that, first and foremost, I should have initiated the complaint, which I failed to do; not once did I feel that all these symptoms were due to insulin or low blood sugar. Furthermore, there was no blood sugar test then.

Doctors had advised me to carry some sugar with me in my pocket and to consume the sugar if and when I had hypoglycemic symptoms. But as I was in class, I was afraid of being caught eating. Moreover, I cannot remember my father informing the teachers about my condition. All the more, my parents and most other adults at that time knew little about diabetes, its symptoms, or how to control the condition.

I feel the fault lies with me because I should have there and then explained the symptoms that arose after eleven or so to my parents. They, in turn, would have informed the doctors. Moreover, my parents were unaware of what an insulin coma was like until I attained adulthood.

Chapter 7

Keeping a Record

As a diabetic, the doctors advised me to test my urine sugar and keep a record of the color. I did not write the color as such but in plus signs. For me, this method of testing was tedious and time-consuming. Just imagine, one has to collect the urine every time for a test by taking a test tube, adding an inch of Benedict solution, putting in eight drops of urine, mixing the two, and heating it over a spirit lamp. Doing this once is bad enough. Just imagine doing it two or three times a day.

Fig. 5. Spirit lamp

Fig 6 Glass syringes and metal needles

Being bored and lazy, I had the inevitable happen. I simply wrote down the color just by feeling my mood and my bodily condition. For instance, if I felt a bit aggressive or depressed or if I were perspiring, I knew the sugar level was low so I wrote down my supposition, a risky guess. I often think that if this complicated testing method were still in use today, most diabetics would fail to carry out these tests. What's more for those who are at work!

Insofar as lessons were concerned, most of the days in school passed without my understanding what was taught, especially so in the latter half of the day. Although I was in a mild hypoglycemic state, I used to walk back home, a short distance away. When I returned home, I would be so hungry that I just gulped down the food that my mother cooked. This is bad for a diabetic. Doctors and nutritionists currently advise that a whole meal should be divided into smaller portions to be consumed in staggered amounts to prevent a sudden uptick in blood sugar levels.

But my mother and I had no such advice or knowledge from medical personnel. When I had these hypo symptoms, the thought of just filling my belly with food was uppermost in my mind. I feel that the brain sends a signal that the body is very deprived of sugars. That is why it makes one load himself with whatever is edible. This has happened to me even recently.

Recently, on or about October 3, 2013, when I felt that I was going into hypo, I tested my blood sugar. The reading was 1.8 mml (very low sugar). The craving for sugar was there. I drank a packet of less-sugar chrysanthemum tea and took some sarsi together with a bit of food. About two hours later, when I tested the blood sugar, the reading was 20.9 mml. This is an attestation of what I stated regarding apportionment of food or drinks for a diabetic.

The advice given by the doctors to me in 1957 and later was not to consume sweet drinks, rice, fruits like apples or oranges, and other sweet stuff. From my experience, all these can and may be taken in a portion commensurate with the type of work a person is doing, the kind of lifestyle, and so on. Recalling the school days after gulping down and relishing in these foods, when I tested the urine sugar in the evenings, I remember the readings being high.

Regarding the amount of insulin I was administered in those days, the dosage was high. I do not remember precisely the units administered, but at one stage, I was injected with between eighty to one hundred units of PZI, which was later changed to Lente. These two types of insulin were administered only once a day, usually in the mornings before breakfast.

I eventually told my father about the lethargy and inability to focus I was experiencing at school in the afternoons; he approached the doctors to sort out this issue. The doctors then changed the timing of the injections from morning to evening. I had to have the injections in the afternoon after I had returned from school.

My father used to go to his office in a trishaw (rickshaw). Therefore, after returning from school and having lunch, I too got into the three-wheeler to be taken to the town clinic. My father was dropped off at his office first.

After the injection, I would return home by bus. The nurses at the clinic in town, because of my daily visits and young age, used to tease me by saying that my arm was a pincushion.

CHAPTER 8

Against the Physician's Advice

Insofar as diabetes was concerned, my parents, especially my father, were not well informed. In 1957 and even many years later, knowledge of this disease was minimal. For most people, diabetes meant counting your days to the grave. This was imprinted in minds.

The contents in this paragraph and others are repeated to impress upon readers conditions then and now about good knowledge on diabetes.

Presently, we have so much information on diabetes via television, the Internet, radio, and other mass media. The media provides a lot of valuable information on avoidance, exercise, diet, and so forth, so much so that one is never at a loss to get precisely whatever knowledge he needs. My father, however, could not resort to many sources besides the doctor's advice.

In the latter part of 1957, I think, my father, out of pity for me, spoke to my physician, Dr. Wong Lunking. He asked him if I could be put on pills. The physician replied with a firm no. As if to console my father, Dr. Wong stated that this disease was quite common with youngsters in the United States. I presume my father resorted to this because, at this time, it was very painful for him to see me being injected with long and hard metal needles. We did not have the disposable syringes and needles that are available now. These needles were reusable, and at times, it was extremely painful when they pricked the skin. Moreover at the hospital, the same needle, after being sterilized, was used over and over again.

The glass syringes and needles at the hospital were sterilized by being boiled. This was a very time-consuming process. Seeing the pain I was undergoing my father also in 1957 took me to see a Chinese traditional doctor 'sinseh' who after taking my pulse reading prescribed some herbs. I took this together with the insulin injections. But there was neither any improvement in my condition nor a cure as my father had hoped.

1) Used since late 1970's

2) Pens from late 1980's

3) Novo mix

Flex pen used since 2012

Fig. 7

In figure 6 are pictures of syringes used in 1957. I hope readers are able to closely examine the pictures and draw their own conclusions of the pain I and others then endured in the early years. In fact, I was injected with these metal syringes until the 1970s.

Toward the latter part of December 1957, my father, against the physician's advice, decided to send me to Singapore to be treated by a different doctor. I was to be put on pills only. Arrangements were made whereby my mother was to accompany me to stay at the house of my uncle, Mr. Sivapragasam, at Sturdee Road.

My cousin Viswanathan, a teacher, took me to the hospital. I wish to apologize because I do not remember many of the names and places in Singapore. But I do know we had to take a bus to get to the hospital.

I was not admitted at the hospital. I was seen by a doctor, who spoke to my mother. And then he prescribed some pills. I was not given any injections. The doctor saw me a few times, and the dosage of the pills was increased gradually. This continued for about a month. The doctors felt the dosage could not be increased anymore. After a stay of nearly a month in Singapore, they decided to send me back home.

During the one-month stay in Singapore, being deprived of insulin injections, I was a total wreck as far as my energy and enthusiasm were concerned. I had no appetite and no interest in food. Even walking felt like a burden. After being a very active diabetic, I became a very docile one.

I kept to myself, reading and practicing a lot of arithmetic. I did not complain to my mother nor to anyone else about my lack of energy. I now think that my mother sensed that my condition was getting worse. Communication with my father was difficult, as there were no house phones nor handheld phones then.

CHAPTER 9

Journey Back Home

After a month of treatment, the doctor in Singapore, knowing that my condition had deteriorated, advised my mother and I to return home. I think he prepared a letter giving details of the treatment I had undergone for the month. On the day I was to leave Singapore by train, I was injected with about fifty units of soluble insulin. This is considered a very high dose; at that time, I'm very sure my blood sugar and ketone levels must have gone up extremely high. This was confirmed later.

On the morning I got into the train with my mother, I was just like a semidead lad being dragged onto the train. There was no feeling of elation to return home because I could feel my health deteriorating. In the meantime, my father had already been informed of our departure and time of arrival. At about noon, we arrived at the Seremban railway station. My uncle, the taxi driver, was there to pick my mother and I up.

CHAPTER 10

Fears and Tears at the Station

Just after I got off the train and onto the platform, I felt very faint and nauseated. Then I just collapsed. Even today, I visualize my mother wailing and my uncle carrying me and putting me into the car. The next thing I remembered was being at the clinic.

I say "remembered" because I could only hear voices and the movement of the trolley. My father had arrived in the meantime. At this time, I had gone into a diabetic coma, hyperglycemia caused by excessive rise in the blood sugar (ketone level then). I was unconscious. My parents later related whatever happened during this time to me.

My father informed me that Dr. Wong gave him a tongue-lashing for not having heeded his advice to not put me on pills. My father later told me that Dr. Wong angrily told him, "You have killed your son." It was then that my father profusely apologized to him and pleaded with him to save my life.

Later my father had to face some lambasting from my mother for failing to heed the doctor's advice and consequently bringing about this situation.

CHAPTER 11

Admission to the Hospital

I was then taken in an ambulance to the hospital. I was put on drips and restarted on insulin. The whole procedure, as was in 1957, was repeated. My urine sugar was tested every few hours, and the nurses recorded the results on a chart. The doctors then prescribed the necessary dosage.

My condition improved drastically after a few days. While the drips were on, I was not allowed to consume water in the normal manner. I could only take spoonfuls of water even though I felt extremely thirsty.

What about my studies? When I was diagnosed with diabetes in 1957, I was in standard (primary) five. Then in 1958, I was in primary six. I had already missed a month of schooling while I was in Singapore, and on admission again in my hometown, I missed another two or three weeks of schooling, a total of about seven weeks.

This was of great concern to me, mainly for the reason that, at that time, all the students in primary six had to sit for an assessment examination. Among the subjects tested was one on intelligent quotient (IQ). This examination was a very competitive one. There were three grades: A, B, and C. Those who obtained a grade C went to a special school known as post primary school where, other than the normal subjects, they studied vocational subjects and trade skills. For parents then, vocational subjects were a no-no, and they were not well-accepted. Today, vocational subjects are in great demand as they help create a skilled workforce.

I had already missed about two months of education. The only subject I did practice in Singapore was arithmetic. I was way behind in all the other subjects.

After my return to school, I had a lot of catching up to do. I had to seek help from fellow students by copying notes from them. Conditions then were vastly different. Today, insofar as education at any level is concerned, there is never a shortage of workbooks, revision notes, and other educational materials ranging from primary one to university. In 1958, photocopying was unheard of. So whatever had to be copied had to be done by hand.

If I remember correctly, I returned home from the hospital in early or mid-February 1958. The public examination was held in November of every year before the December school holidays. With my energy and enthusiasm back, I had to make up for lost time. And this I did fervently. Every evening after my bath and prayers, I used to sit in my room and read aloud whatever I wanted to remember and memorize such things as dates in history as well as other subjects. I did not go out to play, as was usual. At times, I used to work out the IQ papers that our teachers gave to us.

My hard work paid off as I obtained a grade B; I missed out on grade A by about eleven points. My parents were happy, but I was not. But considering all the difficult episodes of 1957, I think I did fairly well.

CHAPTER 12

Self-Administered Insulin

My father was concerned that I had to travel by two buses every day to be at the hospital for my daily insulin injections. I'm not sure whether he spoke to my doctors and suggested that the injection be administered at home, but later, my father, through his friend who was a storekeeper at the hospital, managed to get sterilizing equipment, syringes, and needles. He was also able to get test tubes and a spirit lamp for testing the urine sugar.

My father was the first one to inject me with insulin daily. Later, my eldest sister took over this chore. I was not all smiles when I was injected. The whole process was a very painful one. The needles were long and broad, and the insulin had to be injected subcutaneously (under the skin).

From the 1950s until the 1970s or thereabouts, disposable syringes, as are used today, were not in use. (I refer you to figure 6 again.) If the length, size, and circumference of needles then and now are considered, readers may understand the degree of pain that patients then had to endure. The needles to be used again and again had to be sharpened, so my father purchased a grindstone for this purpose. I attest to the pain endured back then because I am now injecting myself with disposable pen needles. I don't even feel the needle entering the skin.

In figure 7, I have also shown the disposable syringes I used in the 1970s and the disposable syringes I'm using now.

CHAPTER 13

1959: A Fractured Right Wrist, Jaundice, and Shingles

In 1959, I was in form one (secondary one), also at King George V School. The primary school I studied in was adjacent to the secondary school. At the back of the government quarters I was staying in, there was and is a small field. Nearly every evening, my neighbors and I used to play football or indulge in some other activities.

While I was playing one day, I tripped over the ball and landed awkwardly on my right wrist, palm bent inward. My right hand from the wrist onward started swelling. I returned home and took my bath. My parents came to know of this injury. But toward late evening, the swelling got worse, and the pain was unbearable.

I was then sent to the admission room at the hospital. The hospital assistant put my right arm in a sling and gave me a painkiller, some pills. I was asked to come for admission the next day. After an X-ray, I was admitted to the first-class ward because I had to have surgery for the injury. This ward was at a place called Gun Hill.

The night before surgery, the attendant inserted a rubber hose into my anus, and he poured what looked like a soapy solution through the hose. It was a laxative.

The next morning, my bowels were emptied. Later the same day, I was taken in an ambulance to the operation theater. At the theater, I was given an intravenous injection, presumably an anesthetic. The registrar, Dr. Ratnasingham, who would perform the repair, told me to count up to ten. Before I could complete the count, I was in another world, freed of any pain or knowledge of the environment.

After about two days in the ward, I was discharged and then returned home and later to school. My right hand was put in a plaster of paris (POP). As a right-hander, at school, I was unable to write with the bulky POP. Furthermore, I was advised not to lift or carry heavy things.

So the only alternative was to use my left hand to write and to do any other work deemed necessary, such as having a bath and so on. We did not have showers then, so I had to use my left hand to lift buckets of water from a tub and pour the water over my body. The writing was atrocious. Teachers understood.

In 2011, when the class of 1963, ex-students of the same form five, had a gathering, one of my classmates, Mr. Mahadevan, told other students about my determination at school in spite of the fractured right wrist and my struggle to write with my left hand. I feel he was appreciative of my determination and efforts to keep studying and attending classes. The other reason he related this was because all the ex-students were meeting me for the first time after forty-seven years, and they even inquired about the diabetes.

The cast was removed two weeks later after an X-ray had been done. Again I was advised not to lift heavy things.

In the same year, I had an attack of jaundice and later shingles. For both these afflictions, my mother used traditional medication. The shingles appeared on my back. I had a fever, and when I went to school, my only fear was that my fellow students might pat me on the back. It was sore.

If a diabetic is infected with any disease, blood sugar levels will rise, more so for a juvenile (brittle diabetic). When I was a child, this was made even worse by the fact that there were no glucometer tests to get precise readings for blood sugar. Whenever I had an infection and did a self-examination, my urine sugar level was always high.

CHAPTER 14

1960: An Error of Judgment

In 1959, my insulin dosage was readjusted, taking infections into consideration. In 1960, for the first time, I commenced administering insulin injections on my own. I was in form two. I felt more at ease with my condition and dealing with it. Even if I felt pain while injecting, it was my own doing rather than either my father or my sister. But in the same year too, a few weeks later, I erred in dosage calculation. This error continued for quite a long time.

What was this error? Each marking in the scale of the glass syringe I was using measured five units of insulin. But I mistook each unit to represent four units of insulin and consequently I was dosing myself with many extra units of insulin over and above that prescribed.

If I were only on a daily dosage of eighty units of insulin, I should have drawn out five times sixteen unit markings on the syringe. Instead, I had been drawing four times twenty unit markings. This is only an example.

After a few months, I realized my error. I dared not tell the doctors, nurses, or even my father. I was very silly. What did I do instead? I readjusted the dosage to the proper level. The reduction, I think, was about twenty units, and I did not impose the decrease in a gradual manner, as I should have. The urine sugar level was erratic, but being young and ignorant, I did not realize the seriousness of this. Now I am absolutely sure that, due to this the ketone and blood sugar levels would have increased drastically and this was confirmed later.

One weekend, my cousins from Kuala Lumpur came to visit my family. Then all of us, including my brothers and sisters, went in their cars to the beach resort at Port Dickson, about twenty miles away from my home town for a picnic and swim. When I was in Port Dickson, I had reminiscences of the 1958 episode in Singapore. I felt the sick feeling of an impending disaster. Though one would feel elated going to a seaside resort under normal circumstances, for me, it was just the opposite. But everyone else had a good time. We had meals and drinks prepared from home, and later in the evening, all of us returned home.

Over a period of time, my urine sugar level had already gotten high due to my sudden readjustment of the insulin dosage. This was made even worse at the seaside when I consumed food and drinks not recommended for diabetics.

The evening after we returned home from the seaside, for the second time I had a hyperglycemic attack. Unlike the incident in 1958, I was aware of what was happening. But I felt very nauseated and threw up whatever I had consumed. I could not stand upright. I just slumped down in a chair.

Seeing my state, my father immediately took me to the hospital, and I was admitted once again. This time, as all the first- and second-class wards were full, I was sent to the third-class ward just opposite the second-class ward. I was put on drips for a few hours.

I was not allowed to consume any drinks. I felt thirsty, but the doctor told my parents to give me only a few spoonfuls of water. Having a hyperglycemic condition results in extreme thirst, but the moment a lot of fluid is consumed, it brings the liquids back up. Finally, after a few hours of saline drips, I was able to resume normal consumption of liquids but in measured amounts. Later, I was transferred to the second-class ward.

By now, the nurses were already very familiar with me and my condition. As I was so often in and out of the wards, the nurses made fun of me by saying that the hospital was my second home. I was warded for about two weeks.

CHAPTER 15

Another Mistake Due to Laziness

My glass syringes and metal needles had to be sterilized daily. I found this to be very time-consuming more so on weekdays when I had to go to school. In 1960, I was fourteen years old and in form two. Due to ignorance and laziness, I took an easy way out. I just washed the syringes and needles in cold water. The least I could have done was to dip the needles in alcohol.

The outcome was that a ball of puss (carbuncle) appeared on my left thigh. I was again taken to the town clinic. The nurse cut open the wound, and they drained out the puss. After the wound was treated and patched up, I was given an injection of penicillin prescribed by the doctor who examined the wound. Then I passed out. I was revived, and the doctors said I was allergic to penicillin. The concerned doctor knew I had been taking penicillin injections for the treatment of my tonsils.

However, even now I feel I passed out because of the shock of seeing so much puss, and second, I was weak as a result of a high sugar level. The scar from this wound is still on my leg. I had to go for daily dressing of the wound for about a week.

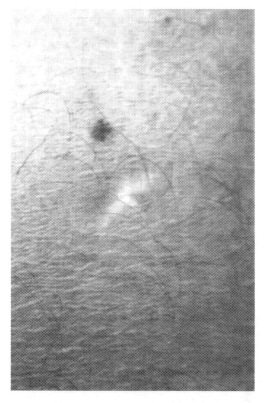

Fig. 8. Picture of scar

1963

In 1963, I had to appear for another very important examination. I was in form five, and those in this form had to sit for the Senior Cambridge Examination ("O" level) set by the University of Cambridge. At this time, those who sought employment in the civil service had to get through this examination.

As my sugar level was still erratic, the new and able physician Dr. Christopher readjusted my dosage by including soluble insulin. The new combination of soluble and PZI provided good control of my sugar level. However, a new problem emerged, as during the first two hours after being injected with soluble insulin, I often had to endure low blood sugar attacks. These were sometimes very severe. When the attacks came, I used to perspire, my head would shake as if I was going into a fit, and I would grind my teeth as if I was angry.

This new dosage was introduced to me in the midst of the school term. I had to be admitted and miss lessons again. This time, however, I brought along some revision notes and books. As I had ample time at my disposal, reading helped, especially in history (a few topics I looked into appeared as questions in the examination).

As in 1959, I was once again admitted to the first-class ward up at Gun Hill. I had a very good elderly friend and uncle by the name of Jansz. He was a very jovial man and had plenty of jokes. He would make the other patients laugh too.

After a stay of a week or two, I was discharged. After being discharged, one evening, being eager to see Mr Jansz, I cycled all the way from my house on Hose Road(now Jalan Zaaba) to the ward at Gun Hill, a distance of about two and a half miles.

I probably burned a lot of calories cycling a steep gradient to reach the first-class ward. After meeting and talking to Mr. Jansz, I returned home. This was in the evening. I guess the sugar level may have dropped considerably the following day, as I went into a hypoglycemic coma and was readmitted in the same ward and same bed next to Mr. Jansz. All the patients had a good laugh.

When I was readmitted, Dr. Christopher made further adjustments to my dosage. The soluble insulin could be mixed together with PZI, the long-acting insulin, but if it were, it would not be very effective because this would also be converted into a slow-acting dose. So I was advised to inject myself twice, first the soluble and subsequently the PZI. I had to endure all pain from the long metal needles and often blunt ones resulting from overuse.

I sat for the form five examination in 1963 and got through, though not with very good results. In 1960, my father had to quit the government quarters at Jalan Kiernan. We had to move to a terrace house as tenants. In order to bear the costs, my father sought employment in the private sector. For a good period of time, even after his retirement, we were fortunate because the government reemployed him in the land office at various districts and states.

CHAPTER 16

Into the Teaching Service

Around 1964, the government embarked upon a program to recruit a good number of teachers to teach various subjects, including industrial arts and physical education. At this time, I was privately studying for the higher school certificate examination.

When this proposal by the government arose, I applied, in part because this was the most suitable job for me in the physical condition I was in. Second, this was not a full-time course where students were put in a college for two years. If that had been the case, I do not think I would have taken this offer. This teacher training course was a two year course, that is, from 1965-1966.

This course was unique because the trainee teachers were posted to various schools all over the country, and on weekends, they had to attend lectures delivered by experienced teachers and lecturers at particular centers. During the school vacations, we had to go to other states, stay in school hostels, and be instructed by lecturers from colleges and universities.

As for me, I was very fortunate, as I was posted to the Chan Wa Secondary School, situated along Temiang Road, in my hometown. I reported to the school in February 1965. I was in this school until my optional retirement on January 1, 1992.

As for the weekend courses, these were held at King George V Secondary School, my alma mater. This was a walking distance from my home. Often I used to cycle to the school. The teaching course was a two-year course, at the end of which all of us had to sit for an examination.

We were posted to various states during school vacations. On the one hand, it was a learning experience because we had an opportunity to see places we had never seen before for the first time. Second, we got to know and meet new friends and colleagues of the same profession from all over the country. But for me, traveling, especially by train, was very bothersome. Other than my clothes, I had to bring along a tripod stand, an aluminum container, and a spirit lamp to sterilize my glass syringe and needles.

An iron smith made the tri pod stand as per the instructions of my father. It was different from the ones used at science laboratories at school because two pieces of metal rod were welded together on the surface so the aluminum container could be placed on the top.

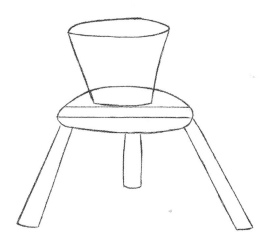

Fig. 9. Sketch of tri pod stand as used then.

Every time during the in-service courses, I had to carry the above mentioned. At the hostels, I used to get up earlier than the other trainees so I could collect water for boiling the syringe and needles. I made sure I boiled the glass syringe and needles, as I did not want to repeat the 1960 episode of using unsterilized needles and syringes.

For me, going for the in-service courses was not a pleasure. The thought of carrying this additional bulk, together with the concern about the kind of foods available that were not suitable for a diabetic, was uppermost in my mind. In addition, I did not carry the equipment necessary for testing the urine sugar level. So at all times and during the whole course, my sugar level was high. I attest to this because I could feel it in my system.

Today, going to another place for a vacation or any other purpose is a breeze for a diabetic because all he needs to bring along is a pen filled with insulin vials or just a disposable pen, a glucometer, and a spirit swab. That is all. Once again, I leave it to the readers to come to their own conclusions as to comparing conditions then and now. Please refer to figures (6 and 7).

As for the food and beverages served during the courses, the hostel canteen caretakers just prepared the same food for all the trainees. Nobody ever asked about sugar intake in beverages; I presume that's because they assumed that all of us, being young, were healthy.

In relation to the government service, all of us had to undergo a medical examination, including a chest X-ray. My father and I were concerned that a negative medical report disclosing my illness would result in the teaching service rejecting my application. So my father and I spoke to Dr. Christopher, and he then told his registrar, Dr. Krishnan, what to write.

So Dr. Krishnan wrote these very words: "This lad is a diabetic, but the physician is of the opinion that he is fit for government service as his diabetes is adequately controlled." I submitted this with the application forms. Later, I was called for the interview and subsequently selected.

CHAPTER 17

A Thud

In 1966, I was dressed up to go to school one morning. I had no transport of my own, so I used to get a lift from Mr. Senathipathy, who was staying a few meters away and was also teaching at Chan Wa Secondary School. As I was waiting outside for his car, my mother and sister heard a thud. When they came out to investigate, they found me lying on the concrete. I had gone into an insulin coma (hypoglycemia). I was then sent to my second home, the hospital, and returned home the same day.

I became a qualified teacher in 1967. I was asked to teach my optional subjects, English language, history, and physical education, a nonoptional subject.

ICED MILO

Around 1970 or 1971, once again due to my carelessness and negligence, I brought about a serious situation that could possibly have caused brain damage. As I was actively involved in games and carrying weights, I used to enjoy a cup of iced milo. (a nutritious chocolate malt drink) I used to mix a cup of strong milo and then put the cup in the freezer. Later, when the milo was frozen, I used to dig up the frozen milo with a spoon and enjoy the ice cream.

Milo as a drink is sweet. Under normal circumstances, I would not consume it, but on the days I exercised and burned calories, then and only then would I resort to consumption as such.

Being too cautious so as not to raise my blood sugar level, I injected myself with an extra dose of soluble insulin. The error I made was that I should have first tested my urine sugar level. If the result had been negative, I might not have given myself this dose.

Sure enough, after a while, I became like a zombie, staring at the things in the storeroom. I think it was my mother who, knowing the symptoms of hypoglycemia, quickly alerted my sister and brother-in-law, both doctors, about my condition, which triggered a violent reaction in me. I ground my teeth and became very aggressive. I think about five people had to restrain me

My brother-in-law, Dr. Asohandran Arasaradnam, with the help of others, forced sweet drinks into my mouth. It took me about an hour to recover. When I recovered, lying on a cot, I realized I had bitten my tongue. It was very sore and had blue-black marks. Whenever I ate spicy food, I experienced a burning sensation. I had to swallow, not chew, the food.

The following day, I think it was a Saturday, I returned to school. My memory was so badly affected that I could not even remember the names of my students I was close with. I had to ask students to repeat their names. It took me about two days to return to my normal physical condition.

Later, I had similar attacks, but less severe. The culprit for these hypo attacks was the soluble insulin. It often resulted in a violent reaction, in the sense that the hypo attack would come so quickly that I had no time to think of consuming something sweet. Sudden shaking of the head, grinding teeth, and aggression were common.

During this period, I was not advised to lower my soluble insulin dosage if my urine sugar level were negative or had a low reading. Only now I realize that, had I then lowered the soluble insulin dosage by a few units, such frequent attacks could have been avoided.

Either in 1971 or 1972, an amusing incident occurred in school when I was a teacher. I was taking a physical education class at the basketball court. I must have burned quite a few calories. Suddenly, I had a blackout, a hypo attack. I was told that I had fallen down on the ground and lay flat. The students must have alerted the school principal. Fortunately, a doctor by the name of Dr. Khoo was staying just opposite the school. He was alerted. He came over and injected me with glucose. I recovered immediately. The administrative assistant, Mr. Choong Yoon Thiam, joked, saying that they thought I was demonstrating an exercise to the students.

I later returned to the class to continue teaching. Mr. Choong also joked that I was like a roly-poly or "never fall" doll. He used a Chinese name, "Pu Dau Ngng," which means "no fall doll."

It is true that, after a hypo attack, I would recover quickly after being given a sweet drink or glucose. People not aware of diabetic conditions would be surprised. But this was not always the case.

In fact, on January 1, 2010, the same batch of students had a reunion lunch at the Min Kok restaurant in town. One of the students, a girl, joked about this incident. All of us had a good laugh.

CHAPTER 18

Koch's Infection

Either toward the end of 1969 or early 1970, I found that my urine sugar level was constantly on the rise. The level was more on the yellow side of the scale (+++) than lower. I became a regular jogger, running about five or five and a half miles at a time, and normally after such a burn-up of calories, my sugar level would drop. But strangely, this was not happening. What was even more intriguing was that I was losing weight. My concern was not about the weight loss, which I would gladly accept, but the high sugar level.

Then my sister, Dr. Rajeswari, who at that time was a medical officer at the new General Hospital, now known as Hospital Tuanku Jaafar, referred me to my physician, Dr. Christopher. Dr. Christopher told me to take a chest X-ray. Later, when the X-ray was shown, it confirmed that I was infected with tuberculosis, or Koch's infection. The X RAY showed that there was a scar the size of a ten-cent coin. Fortunately, the sputum showed negative results. Otherwise, I would have been put in an isolation ward and away from teaching for some time.

I was admitted to the first-class ward on the seventh floor. The insulin dosage had to be increased as a consequence of the Koch's infection. I was also injected daily with streptomycin injections for a period of six months, and I was also told to take a few pills, green in color.

Every day I used to go to the hospital to be injected with the streptomycin injections. X-rays of my lungs were often taken to monitor the progress of the treatment.

CHAPTER 19

At the Language Institute

In 1971, teachers had to attend an intensive Malay language course at the Language Institute at Pantai Valley, Kuala Lumpur. The course was for about a month. I was chosen to attend the course during the second semester. One day while I was at the canteen, without any warning, I had a hypo attack and became unconscious. The next thing I knew, I found I was at the university hospital nearby. I suppose one of my colleagues who knew about my condition must have alerted the authorities.

Later, my brother-in-law, A. Vijayaratnam, who had married my eldest sister, Sarojini, came to the hospital to take me back to his house. Still today I do not know who informed him. He was a police officer with the rank of superintendent of police. After having rested at the house, I returned to the institute. My brother-in-law sent me.

While I was attending the course, I was still administering the streptomycin injection on my own. I had no choice. This injection could not be discontinued. The fact that I had the hypo attack could be attributed to two reasons. One was that my dosage had been increased at the onset of the Koch's infection. Second, as the condition was improving, the insulin dosage had to be reduced.

SURGERY ON TONSILS

I had tonsils on both sides of my throat that often swelled. The last straw occurred in 1973 when both the tonsils were so swollen that there was hardly a passageway for solid food to pass through. I gargled salt water in the hope of reducing the swelling to some extent, but it was to no avail. For me especially, it was a problem. On the one hand, any infection would cause an increase in sugar level. On the other hand, as I was on insulin, I had to consume food for obvious reasons, but in this condition, I couldn't take any solid food. It was a dilemma.

Fortunately, at that time, another brother-in-law of mine, Dr. Asohandran, was the registrar for the state surgeon, Mr. Kunanayagam. After making an appointment, my brother-in-law took me to see Mr. Kunanayagam. When my mouth was opened, he could see the tonsils, swollen, infected, and reddish in color. The surgery was not done and could not be done immediately because of the swelling. So I was given antibiotics to bring the swelling down. After that treatment, a day was fixed for the surgery. I opted to do the surgery during the school vacation in August so that students' lessons would not be interrupted. The surgery was done superbly in 1973. To this day, I owe my gratitude to Mr. Kunanayagam, the surgeon, and my brother-in-law Dr. Asohandran.

Dr. Christopher, the physician who was attending to me, was full of praise for Mr. Kunanayagam. I was given antibiotics, and the wounds healed very well. I was discharged from the ward a week later.

CHAPTER 20

Change in Insulin Type

Life went on fairly smoothly for some years. However, sometime in the late 1970s, despite having sufficient and proper control of food and regular exercise, my urine sugar level turned erratic again. This was a cause for concern. I spoke to my sister, Dr. Rajeswari. She stated rightly that it could be due to resistance to soluble insulin and PZI. My sister then took me to see Dr. Richard Lim, a private practitioner who was at one time a physician at the General Hospital. Dr. Richard Lim had also attended to me at the hospital.

Upon seeing me, Dr. Richard Lim confirmed what my sister had suspected earlier. So he put me on a new type of insulin (human insulin of DNA origin). It went by the name of Actrapid (fast-acting) and Monotard (slow- and long-acting). I had to administer both these separately twice a day, as I had been doing with my previous two insulins. I was started on a low dosage. I had to increase the dosage as time passed by.

This new insulin suited me very well. At this time, for the first time in my life, I started using disposable syringes. I felt like I had won a lottery. The needles and syringe were slim and well calibrated. There was no necessity to worry about a mistaken calibration, and the best part was that I did not have to boil the needles and syringes. They were disposable.

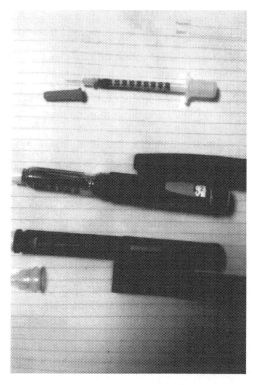

please refer to Fig. 7 page 19

Later on, in 1991, my sister referred me to Dr. Thayaparan, the new state physician. He was a very kind and wonderful doctor, and he continued to attend to me until 2011 when he was transferred to Port Dickson. After listening to my history and looking at all the previous blood test results from the hospital records, he was full of praise for the manner in which I was managing the illness. On hearing his words I told Dr Thayaparan that the discipline I had was perhaps being very young and being told by the physicians on the do's and don'ts I took the advice without any doubts.

I then remarked that, since I had gotten the disease at the age of eleven, and being young just absorbed and followed all advice given by the doctors. He replied that it was not so and added further, "Do you know how many people who were diagnosed with diabetes at more or less the same age died at the age of eighteen, twenty, and so forth? The reason is because they did not have the discipline and nature to have strict control over their food intake and/or exercise their bodies." He knew I used to exercise because he himself had seen me walking at about four in the afternoon or so.

At about this time, I was having problems with my bladder. Dr. Thayaparan referred me to a surgeon, Mr. Paul Silvindoss, who, after examining my prostrate, confirmed that it was enlarged. I was prescribed some pills, and this helped to shrink the prostrate. Later, I was referred to Professor Dzulkifli at the National University of Malaysia at Cheras, Kuala Lumpur. Presently, I seek treatment at this hospital, though, thankfully, it is just once a year.

CHAPTER 21

1984-1988 (Embarking on Reading of Law)

From 1984 until 1988, my friends and fellow teachers from different teaching institutions took up legal studies on a part-time basis. The ultimate goal, of course, was to qualify as lawyers, and to do this, all of us had to sit for the University of London (external) LLB examination. This course consisted of the Intermediate and parts 1 and 11, a total of three parts. A candidate had to get through all his papers before he could proceed to appear for the next part. It was tough, as we were all full-time teachers.

Most of us used to attend lectures at night at the Mona Tuition Centre, a center providing tuition for school students. This center was let to us by Mr. Krishna Dallumah, the administrator and teacher at the center. Mr. Krishna is now a very well-established practicing lawyer.

Practicing lawyers delivered the law lectures, and some were law students studying in London who were on vacation. Most of us got through the LLB examination but at different times. I passed my part II final examination in 1988. Considering the fact that we were full-time employees, nearly all of us obtained the professional degree from a very well-established and well-known university.

CERTIFICATE IN LEGAL PRACTICE (CLP)

It was one thing to get through the external examination, but to practice in a court of law as an advocate, we had to sit for and pass the Certificate in Legal Practice (CLP) examination. This examination and course was specifically tailored to meet the demands of the many students who were sitting for external law examinations and who could not afford to go to London to sit for the bar examination. This bar examination in Malaysia is a very tough one where, in any one year, only about 20 to 25 percent of students get through on the first attempt.

As for me, this course was a great blessing because I was a teacher and could adjust my schedule to cope with the course structure. This CLP course was a full-time course with lectures in the morning and tutorials in the evening. The whole course was for a period of nine months. I skipped the lectures and only attended these on Saturdays, if any. However, I attended all the tutorials, this being mandatory. I was very fortunate because I had two fellow colleagues, Mr. Manian Rajoo and Miss Joanna Wong, teachers who were full-time CLP students. They passed the lecture notes on to me.

Immediately after the last school bell rang at about one ten, I would jump into my car and drive off for lectures and tutorials at the lecture halls at the University of Malaya, Kuala Lumpur. This went on for nine months. Most of my weekends were free.

As I used to inject insulin twice a day, I took along the disposable syringes, insulin vials, and spirit swabs. Every day at about six in the evening, immediately after a lecture/tutorial and before the commencement of the next tutorial, I would run to my car to inject the insulin and, following that, eat the food I had brought along. I used to jab myself twice, once with the Actrapid and then the Monotard. Following this, I would gulp down whatever food I had brought, usually a bun, bread, or biscuits. Then I would rush back to the lecture/tutorial class. All this I did in about six or seven minutes. This is true! My friend Manian Rajoo would attest to this.

The tutorials or lectures would be over by eight or nine, and when I returned home, Manian Rajoo and Joanna Wong would accompany me in my car. Both these colleagues/friends were from the same hometown and attended classes at the Mona Tuition Centre in the early years. Today, Manian Rajoo and Krishna Dallumah, the administrator of the Mona Tuition Centre, are partners in a legal firm under their names, and they are two of the top litigation lawyers not only in my state but perhaps in the whole country. Both are doing very well.

Manian Rajoo, who traveled back home daily with me, knew about my illness and hypo attacks. Whenever I drove back to Seremban after the tutorials, he used to be very alert and kept an eagle eye ever watchful on my driving, observing for erratic actions. To be honest, the so-called dinner I had in the car was not at all sufficient. I ate a little only and quickly too. Often he would advise me to consume the mixed cordial I brought along.

In one incident, I was driving while already going into a hypoglycemic condition; I failed to recognize the highway leading back home. Instead, after the toll, I nearly veered off to the right, heading toward the Agricultural University at Serdang. Even today, Manian Rajoo jokes about this incident.

CHAPTER 22

CLD Orientation

I had gotten through the part II of the LLB examination in 1988. I had also related to matters relating to lectures, tutorials, and the management of insulin and meals at the short break, if it can be called a break.

This course proper was conducted in 1989. Prior to this course, all the students had to attend an orientation course where the students from all over the country could meet all their law lecturers and tutors and get to know them. The law students were mostly adults from different age groups ranging from the young, the middle-aged, and even older.

The orientation course was held on a Saturday. I did not drive to the university. Instead, I parked my car at the Sungai Ujong Recreation Club, a clubhouse about five kilometers away from my house. I was now staying in my own home (which is still my home) at 1480 Rasah Road (now Jalan Rasah). I moved out to the present house in 1984.

For the orientation course, I went along with Joanna Wong. From the Sungai Ujong Club, I got into Joanna's car, which her husband Billy Wong drove. We were taken to the university for the orientation. At one of the lecture halls after the talks by the course administrator, we were served beverages and some light food, such as biscuits and sandwiches, but I made a very serious and stupid mistake of not consuming food to build up the calories.

When everything was over, Billy Wong dropped me at the Sungai Ujong car park where I had parked my car. On reaching my car I suddenly had a strange, depressing and gloomy feeling, sure sign of an imminent hypoglycaemic attack. This is explained in the following chapter.

CHAPTER 23

Very Erratic and Dangerous Behavior Due to Hypoglycemia

Unknown to me, my blood sugar level could have dropped to a dangerous level. Just as I was about to start the car, I had the first inkling that the blood sugar level was very low. I consumed whatever diluted cordial drink I had taken along with me. I even used up the glucose powder I had. It was then that I put myself into a situation that could have endangered not only myself but others, especially the road users.

First and foremost, I should have stayed put in my car and waited for at least twenty minute after consuming the cordial and the glucose powder. In my experience, whenever there is an attack of hypoglycemia and sugar or any sweet drink is given, I feel the level dropping even further; it is only after some time that the condition gradually returns to normal.

But because I was eager to return home fast, I started the engine and drove on. One may wonder why I did not communicate this to either Joanna Wong or Billy. After all, I went to Kuala Lumpur and returned from Kuala Lumpur in Billy's car. Only a person familiar with such a condition would be able to see my face and eyes and know I was about to go into a hypoglycemic attack. The symptoms would have been there, but Joanna and Billy were not familiar with these. Here again, I wish to state from my many experiences that, perhaps due to lack of oxygen to the brain resulting from the lowering of energy (sugar content), I would know I am hypo, but I would not be able to communicate a need for help. In this instance, I was like a zombie handling a dangerous instrument, the car.

I started the engine and drove off. It should be remembered that the distance from the clubhouse to my home was about three miles. As I was driving, my eyes became crossed, first due to my very low blood sugar level and my distorted vision—by this, I mean that I could see the road and vehicles, but I could not see the middle line in the road. So I had to seemingly cross my eyes to align the car with my side of the road. I vaguely remember crossing into the wrong lane. Cars were constantly honking.

But I kept on going. Whatever sweet stuff I had taken earlier still had not seemingly had any effect. My main aim was to reach home as early as possible to get help from my wife. But this was not to be. I, in fact, passed my house and landed in a neighboring housing estate known as Ho Garden. This was about less than a quarter mile away. I was so near my home yet so far from my destination. When I reached Ho Garden, I turned off the car engine and waited. Even in 1989, most of us did not have mobile phones, which were very expensive. By experience, I knew the cordial mixture and glucose would soon take effect, and they did.

The road from the club to my home was not a straight one. I had to pass through a roundabout and three junctions, two of them being main and busy junctions. Finally, I reached home, thanking the Maker that, just as he had created unfavorable conditions for me, he had also seen to it that nothing untoward happened.

While I was driving in this terrible hypoglycemic condition, just after I had left the club and as I was passing the chief minister's (in Malay language, Menteri Besar's) residence, I even had mental time to pray to the Almighty and nature. "If ever, let me get killed, but don't I ever go and knock down an innocent person." Strange as it may seem, this did occur.

A person reading this book may wonder why I go into hypoglycemic attacks so often and expose others and myself to life-endangering situations. My answer is that I am overly cautious about sugar level control and consequently too watchful over the food I consume. Second, being a diabetic for a long period of time, the system has become conditioned to very low sugar levels wherein I am not able to feel or recognize an onset of an attack or hypo state. Consequently, as my sugar level gets even lower, the oxygen supply to the brain is reduced, and the brain is not able to tell my other senses that I have to drink or eat something sweet immediately. It is then that incidents, as explained previously, occur.

To give another example, I once felt perfectly all right, but at the same time, I realized a hypo attack was imminent while I was driving. I had a cordial drink in my car, and I could have taken it at once, but I did not do it. Why? I wanted to return home to test my sugar level.

Fortunately, when I did, the test result was a 1.6 mml reading, a very low and dangerous level. As my body had been conditioned to such levels, I was able to drive home safely. I am not being boastful but silly. As I have mentioned earlier this condition arises because I am too cautious with what I consume be it food or drinks and furthermore I am never physically inactive. These are two essential prerequisites for good control of diabetes. Such incidents have happened many times in the recent past.

After passing the CLP examination in 1991, I took my optional retirement in 1992 at the age of forty-six. To practice in a court of law, every law graduate had to do chambering under a master, usually a senior lawyer with more than seven years of practice. I chambered under the late Mr. Seeralan. After chambering was completed, I was officially called to the bar in 1992, and as a newly qualified lawyer, I worked under two senior lawyers, respectively

However, in 1995, I decided to practice on my own. When you work for somebody, you have to be at his beck and call. I was not young, and furthermore, because of the diabetic condition, I just could not cope with traveling from one place to another, one district to another often to just mention cases. But most importantly, monitoring the sugar level, especially while being in another place, was surely a hindrance. Being a diabetic for a long time prevented me from detecting low sugar levels unless another person was with me and knew my condition.

CHAPTER 24

A Repetition

During the period between 1995 and 1996, I had two or three very serious attacks of hypoglycemia. In one incident, I had just returned home from court. It was about noon. As usual, I had not eaten any food nor taken any other edible stuff. I read the papers, and I was just sitting in the living room waiting for a friend who used to help me with traffic matters. I was still in lawyer's attire, minus the necktie.

I sensed I was due for an imminent attack of hypoglycemia because, as I was reading the newspaper, I was straining to read the words, sometimes becoming cross-eyed. I went to the kitchen to mix some cordial, but I could not do so. I failed to keep my balance. I went to the back door, hit the door, and then fell on a hardened cement bag, which a contractor who previously had done some renovations in the kitchen had left behind. Then I stood up again, staggered, hit the metal railings leading to the washroom and toilet, and fell down again.

The impact of the very hard knocks, maybe two or more times, perhaps shocked me into some sort of recovery, and consequently, I staggered to the hall and then passed out. Just then, my friend Mr. Lim arrived. On seeing me lying unconscious, he rushed to the Mawar (private) hospital nearby and contacted Dr Yeow Thiam Loy, the director and also a then State Assemblyman. And then an ambulance was called to cart me to the hospital. My wife was at work during this time.

At the hospital, I was injected with glucose solution, and I recovered immediately. My sister Dr. Rajeswari, who was working at the General Hospital, upon hearing about me, came to see me. The first person I recognized on waking up was Staff Nurse Mary Nayagam, who had attended to me at the first-class ward in 1970. I presume she was the one who had informed the doctor about my diabetic condition. At that time, I was not wearing a medic alert emblem, as I do now.

The first thing I told Miss Nayagam was that I felt I had had a beautiful dream. It is true! At that moment, the effect of the numerous knocks and falls in the house showed no symptoms. In this particular hypo state, I felt I had had a blissful sleep.

Only a day later did I experience all the pain, especially in my shoulders, arms, and back. Surprisingly, the pain was bearable.

CHAPTER 25

Groan in Pain

On May 16, 2003, at about three in the morning, my wife heard me making strange sounds and noises in my sleep. It was not a dream! My wife, Rajalakshmi, who is so very familiar with the diabetic condition, got up to check on me. I was frothing very badly. As usual, she rushed to the kitchen to mix some cordial and glucose. The hurdle, however, was to force the sweet liquid into a mouth that was frothing and wouldn't even open. If she inserted an object to pry open my mouth, it could damage my teeth.

I was told that she had been trying for more than an hour and I spat out whatever liquid was poured into my mouth. My wife had no alternative but to call for an ambulance. I was taken to the hospital and given intravenous glucose solution.

In my previous incident, I had stated that the whole episode was like a beautiful dream. In this episode, however, it was a total reverse. I was groaning as if in severe pain. I felt my body twisting. Only when I saw the faces of the medical staff was I aware that I was in the hospital. My wife was in the treatment room also. My appearance was so horrible that, upon seeing my wife, the hospital assistant asked me if she was my daughter. Such an insult!

This condition could have been a consequence of being under hypo for a long period of time until detection. Herein is a copy of my admission card and diagnosis cum treatment.

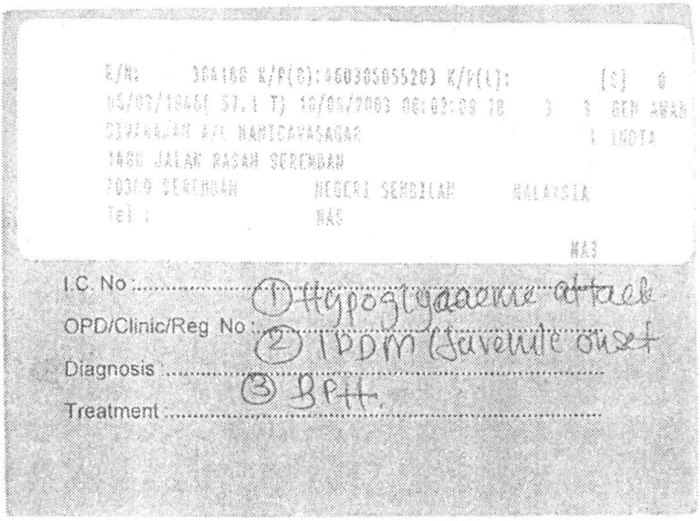

I.C. No: ① Hypoglycaemic attack

OPD/Clinic/Reg. No: ② IDDM (Juvenile onset

Diagnosis:

Treatment: ③ BPH

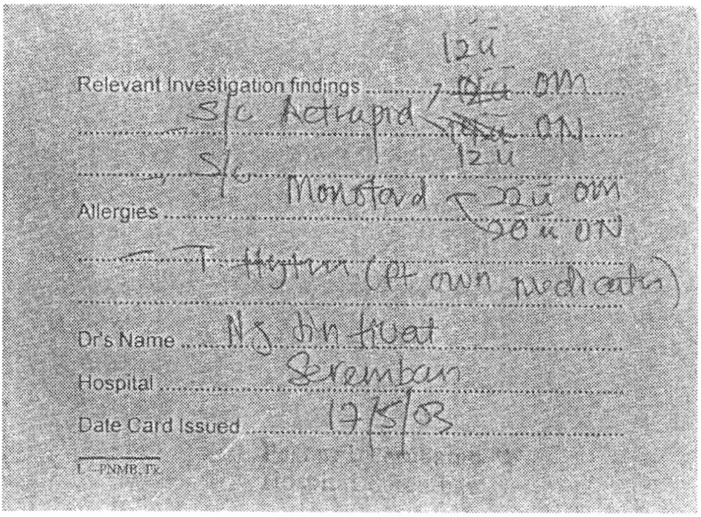

Relevant Investigation findings:

S/C Actrapid 12u OM / 12u ON

S/C Monotard 22u OM / 20u ON

Allergies:

T. Hytrin (pt own medication)

Dr's Name: Ng

Hospital: Seremban

Date Card Issued: 17/5/03

Fig. 10. (Admission card)

I was admitted in the ward for a day. As far as I was concerned, it was just another incident in the life of a diabetic. The card clearly states the reason for admission.

FURTHER INCIDENTS

I shall relate another very similar occurrence without adhering to a chronological sequence. In May or June 2012, at about two in the morning, my wife related to me that she had heard somewhat strange sounds and noises emanating from me. When she tried to wake me up, there was no response. She kept on giving me glucose powder mixed with cordial. She told me that, at one stage, she had wanted to call for an ambulance.

However, fortunately for me, I recovered at about five. Often when I get up after an attack, I feel that I have been put in a strange place, and the first question I normally ask is "What day is it?" or "What time is it?" My guess is that the hypoglycemic condition must have completely erased a part of the conscious memory at least for a few hours.

Previously, maybe sometime in the late 1990s or the early part of 2000, my wife was working as a library assistant at an army camp at Port Dickson. While I was at home, I had gone into a hypoglycemic state. It was about noon. I might have been feeling drowsy, a clear indication of hypoglycemia. I just slept on the cold floor in the living room near the aquarium.

I was asleep until my wife returned from work to find me lying on the floor. When she arrived, it was already about six, and I was still asleep. The effect of the morning dosage of insulin was perhaps wearing off. My wife mixed some cordial, woke me up, and made me drink it. I realized I had wet my shorts. Was it carelessness again?

One of the reasons I often got these attacks in the afternoon was that I used to skip lunch. While working, I would bring along a sachet of three-in-one Ovaltine with me. This was usually mixed at home or brought in a flask. Usually, I would take this drink at about eleven in the morning, as this is the time the blood sugar level takes a dip. However, this is not always possible, especially when I'm in court attending to matters. The second reason is that, if I had exercised the previous evening, the following morning, there was a high probability of the blood sugar level going down.

One may wonder why I have to skip lunch. Dr. Thayaparan advised me to inject myself with five units of Actrapid (fast-acting) insulin just before having lunch. This was a problem while at work, especially when I am in the court or at the court premises. If the blood sugar were already low and I injected myself with this five units, I would definitely go into a hypoglycemic state and become a burden to everyone.

Second, I did not want to inject myself with the extra five units because I had a tendency to put on weight. If the five units were injected, I had to have lunch, which, in turn, would increase my body mass. I spoke to Dr. Thayaparan about this, and he let me skip the noon dose of insulin.

At work, I did not take along my glucometer for two reasons. One was that I often had to park the car in the sun while at work, and once or twice, the glucometer indicated that it had been exposed to the sun for too long. The second and more valid reason was that, as I had only one meter, I did not want to leave it in the office only to find on returning home that I had neglected to bring it along with me. For me, the morning blood sugar test was a must, as this would tell me whether I should either decrease the dose or increase it by a few units, as the physicians advised.

CHAPTER 26

A Fright for the Magistrate

In 1999, I was handling a road traffic matter in the magistrate's court in Seremban, along Jalan Cumming (Cumming Road). In that year, I was in the legal firm of Edmund H.T. Ponniah and Co. Mr. Edmund instructed me to conduct the hearing. Sitting together with me in the court was Salim Bashir, a chambering student under Edmund. Presently, Salim Bashir is a well-established lawyer practicing in the state of Selangor.

The prosecuting officer for this traffic matter was Inspector Ridzuan. Prior to this, I had explained to the prosecuting officer about my illness and especially the state of hypoglycemia.

In the midst of cross-examination of the prosecution's witness, I began to falter and became erratic; my speech was not cohesive. Knowing my diabetic condition, Inspector Ridzuan asked me if I was all right. He rightly did so because I was struggling to put forth my questions. I was slurring.

The prosecuting officer's question and concern triggered an immediate response. I became excited and aggressive and pushed the table I was seated at. The Honorable Magistrate, Mr. Dasuki, not knowing my condition and looking at my facial expression and aggression, immediately jumped up from the bench and adjourned the matter. He then rushed into his chambers.

Later, the prosecuting officer went into the magistrate's chambers to explain the reason for my strange behavior. I have already related that, in a hypoglycemic attack, one of the symptoms is that the patient becomes aggressive, at times extremely so. I would have strength to push the whole table and, not only that, push away anybody who tried to restrain me. On the other hand, in very similar circumstances, if I were to be spoken to gently, without being made excitable, the reaction would generally be the opposite.

After the prosecuting officer had entered the magistrate's chambers, Salim Bashir took the glucose powder I had with me and then went to the canteen just a door away, mixed it with water, and brought it to me. After consuming the glucose drink, I recovered immediately. When the magistrate reappeared in open court, I apologized to him. However, the case was postponed.

This symptom of aggression from a hypoglycemic attack then reminded me of a more serious attack I had when I was staying with my parents. Persons not familiar with symptoms like this would not be able to detect a person's early symptoms of hypoglycemia.

Even if a diabetic were just getting into a hypoglycemic condition, most people would fail to recognize it. They would take it to be his normal behavior. Only those who are close friends, family members, and forewarned, as was Inspector Ridzuan by me, will immediately respond to such symptoms. In the court, this was my only incident.

I wish to state herein that, usually when hypoglycemic symptoms surface, I would feel very normal for quite some time after the onset of hypoglycemia. Consequently, people around who are unfamiliar with or, rather, ignorant of my illness would not realize that my reactions are beyond normalcy. Only those who are aware of my condition would take pains to alert me or give me some sugar-mixed or sugar-coated stuff.

As a legal assistant in the firm of Edmund H. T. Ronniah and Co., I worked for only half the day unless assistance or any other help was needed by Edmund. Sometime in 2002 at about one thirty or so, I reversed my car, getting ready to return home. At this time, I was feeling drowsy, yet I drove on. But fortunately, I did not go far. After driving for about a hundred meters, I did not know what had happened. As my car was on manual drive, it must have stalled. I was on hypo and had gone to sleep. Fortunately, I was just near the office and not on a busy street.

On seeing me slumped in my seat, another lawyer from the same firm, Jayaprakash Rao, who was familiar with my condition, immediately got a drink from a stall nearby and gave it to me. It came with a straw. I was able to drink it, and after a short while, I drove back home.

A very similar incident occurred again in or about the same year and also at the same time of day. This time, I was in the car about to go back home. I was just sitting in the car, perhaps for some time, with the car engine and AC on. Mr. Edmund was just returning to the office. On seeing me and suspecting something, he quietly went into the office and told Jayaprakash Rao about my condition. Jayaprakash rushed to the car, took the cordial drink I had in the car, opened the cap, and gave it to me.

It may seem strange that, as my condition became worse, I could not reach out to open the container's cap to consume the drink on my own. This is the usual occurrence when my blood sugar level dips fast.

In both the previous incidents, a very serious or tragic accident could have occurred, putting innocent lives at risk.

During the years of practice with Edmund, I often used to sit in front of him to assist him either with his matters or translate his submissions from the English to the national language, Bahasa Malaysia. Very often on seeing my expressions, he would quietly tell me that my sugar level was getting low. I wouldn't feel it, but he was able to see it in my face and advise me. He was right.

Edmund first came to know of the hypoglycemic condition in 1997 when I was sharing a room with him at another place. At that time, he was in partnership with Mr. Tee Kim Chan, and the firm was registered under the name of Edmund H. T. Ponniah and Tee. As I was now on my own and did not have a place in town, Edmund was kind enough to let me share his room.

While both of us were in the room, I suddenly became aggressive and pushed the large table I was seated at. I nearly toppled it. Edmund coolly and calmly helped me by getting a sweet drink, and I was my usual self again. I worked with Edmund until 2007 when I ceased practice.

CHAPTER 27

Advice from My Experience

I shall now resort to repetition on what I had stated in chapter 26. I want to enable readers so new diabetics and family members know what they may have to encounter and how to react to a diabetic in a prehypoglycemic state. Whatever symptoms I have been mentioning are all I personally have experienced. Not being a medical doctor, whatever I state is from my own knowledge and experience, and these could perhaps be taken as guidelines.

A diabetic in a prehypoglycemic state may behave very normal, and he would do so until the next stage when he is beginning to go into hypoglycemia. At the prehypoglycemic state itself, never should a diabetic be made excitable or irritable. The best step would be to immediately give him a sweet drink and tell him gently that you feel that he is going into a hypoglycemic state. You should also alert him by saying that there are symptoms of a hypo state in him from observations you've made. Normally, as has happened many times, when it was pointed out to me that I was showing signs of hypoglycemic behavior, I would just brush it off.

Sometimes when I am in the house and my wife tells me, I confirm it by doing the blood sugar test. Nearly every time, my wife is right. Sometimes she just mixes a sweet drink and brings it to me. I drink it. One thing I've noticed is that, when I'm in a hypo state, I often experience a headache in the upper part of the back portion of the head. But as soon as I take the sweet drink, I can actually feel the headache slowly disappearing. This is a sure sign that I was in a hypo state.

However, in spite of so many years of experience, I have also been deceived. I say "deceived" because even when my blood sugar is very high, I used to have a very bad headache on the whole back of my head. At the beginning, I used to think that the blood sugar was low, so I consumed a sweet drink to lower the sugar level. This made it even worse, and the headache would worsen.

In the early 1980s, there was a sports event organized by the school I was teaching at. While I was on duty as a judge for the event, I suddenly started getting the headache. It was severe. Thinking that, as a result of being on duty in the sun and burning off calories, my blood sugar had dipped, I consumed a box of a sweet drink. In fact, the headache became worse, so much so that I finally swallowed four panadols (paracetomol) on an empty stomach but in a staggered manner. At this time, I did not possess a glucometer. Otherwise, I would have brought it along with me before deciding on the next course of action.

If ever you notice a diabetic straining his eyes to read or see a thing or he becomes irritable for a seemingly insignificant matter, understand that he is in a hypoglycemic condition. Without mentioning anything to him, you should mix a sweet drink and quietly give it to him without getting him excited. But bear in mind that not too much of sugar or cordial should be mixed. The normal amount would be to mix about one or two tablespoons of cordial with just a little water so the drink is sweet and at the same time not containing too much sugar content. If and only if my sugar level is very low, my wife uses two tablespoons of cordial together with a teaspoonful of glucose. Conditions may vary for individual diabetics.

Herein I wish to relate another incident that happened in 1965 at the KGV school hostel. I was accepted into the teaching profession in 1965. During the school vacation, all the teacher trainees from the same batch in the state of Negeri Sembilan, where I'm from, had to be put up at the KGV school hostel. Once, after a physical education practical course, we were at the hostel for lunch.

Suddenly, I saw a trainee who was from another district standing up, holding a plate, and hitting away at the plate with a spoon. At that moment, I could clearly see that his eyes were crossed. Only later did I come to know from his friends and later him that he too was a diabetic on insulin and had been afflicted with the disease since the age of twelve. Obviously, after the physical education course, he might have gone into a hypoglycemic state. I presume that he reverted to the normal state after having his lunch. I relate this incident to let readers be informed of the symptoms of a diabetic becoming excitable and cross-eyed, sure signs of hypoglycemia.

I shall also mention another incident that happened to me while I was teaching. In the 1990s, one day as usual, some teachers during their common free period were sitting in the school canteen. The tables were round. I, normally very vocal, just kept quiet. Probably I was in a hypoglycemic state, but I was unaware. One of my very close buddies, Lee Sik Kiong, who knew my condition, made an inquiry about my state. I became excited and banged the table, just like an hysterical person. I bit and ground my teeth. Mr. Lee Sik Kiong, I think, immediately ordered a sweet drink for me. Fortunately, nothing untoward happened.

CHAPTER 28

The Road and Trees Moving Away from Me

On weekends, I would go out for walks and sometimes jog. I would start off from the house and walk right up to Gun Hill, where a reservoir is situated. The old first-class ward of the General Hospital was once situated below the reservoir. Whenever I went for a walk, I would take two small plastic containers filled with glucose powder along with me.

My daily routine was and is even now to inject myself with insulin at about six thirty in the morning. Then, after having my breakfast, I would start off on my walks at about seven thirty.

One morning in 2005, as I was walking up Gun Hill after completing an hour's exercise, I started feeling unsteadiness in my steps. I was dragging my feet. From my many experiences, dragging of the feet while walking is the first sign of a type 1 diabetic being warned of an imminent hypoglycemic attack. Nature forewarned me, but I often did not heed the warning signs.

In my own stubborn manner, I wanted to achieve what I had set out to do, to walk right up to Gun Hill and then back to the house again. Since I was bent on walking, I consumed some glucose powder I had brought along, which I always bring whenever I go out.

I felt better. But walking uphill for about a quarter mile would surely burn up a lot of my already-low calories. Getting up to Gun Hill was one matter. I had to walk down and back to my house. This again would result in a loss of calories. For me, it also meant a low sugar level.

As I was walking down, my feet dragging became worse. I walked unsteadily, and I was being propelled forward. I could not hold back my walk, and this was made worse by the fact that I was walking downhill. Then on a level road, I just stood still. I could see the road, the trees, and other objects in front receding, running away from me. I knew my hypoglycemic condition was very bad. As a diabetic on insulin and one who exercises regularly, this was a sure test for me to see if the sugar level in my blood was decreasing.

Even now, when I go for walks and when I feel in doubt, I test myself by standing still to test my blood sugar level. If I find the objects and road lying ahead of me moving, then I know for sure that I have to take precautionary actions, and that means either to stop completely or consume glucose with some water or other liquid. It seems strange, but the lower the blood sugar level, the faster the path ahead and objects in front will seem to run away from you. This is a sure test for me.

Reverting to my story, although all these warning signs were there, I just continued, as reaching home quickly was my priority. On my downward walk, my hypoglycemic condition got worse. I tried to stand, but I could not. Such was the wobbly and unsteady posture I had.

As I was still walking downhill, I was pulled onward and forward as if by a force, and I crashed facedown. Luckily, I used my hands to break the fall and hence protected my face. My hands and knees were bruised. I just lay on the road. It was very risky because I was lying down in a corner, and vehicles coming down very often fast from Gun Hill would not be able to brake in time.

CHAPTER 29

A Guard to the Rescue

As I was lying on the road, I saw an old car coming in the opposite direction. I was still lying down on the road. Only at the last moment did I sit up and move to the side of the road where there was a grass patch. The car stopped, and out came a Malay man. He inquired on what had happened and I related the whole incident to him.

He was actually a security guard employed by a private company to keep watch at Gun Hill Reservoir. He was on his way up to Gun Hill. I was still in shock. He had his shotgun over his shoulder, and with that, he tried to pull me up. This guard was not a young man. He was a retiree and now employed as a guard. Just as he was about to lift me up, I told him not to because I could see that his build was not enough to lift me up. He tried anyway. What happened? Both of us fell down, me for the second time. I was able to laugh. Seeing my small size, he told me that he assumed I was a lightweight. I told him appearances are often deceptive. I spoke to him in the Malay language, the national language.

To top it all, when he pulled me up, he pulled me up with his shotgun slung over his shoulder. He asked me to get into his car to be taken up to the Gun Hill Reservoir. There, he gave me some water, which I took together with the little glucose I had left. Then he gave me some herbal liquid called *gamat* to locally apply to the injuries I sustained from the fall. I rested for a short while and then walked all the way back home as if nothing had happened. I did not feel any worse, truly a roly-poly doll. Strangely (and this has happened many times after a fall resulting from such an attack), I would recover immediately. I presume it is nature's way. Only later would the pain from the knock and injuries be felt.

A year later, a very similar incident happened. This was also during the course of a walk in the morning. I had already walked for about an hour or so and was on my way back home. I was near an army camp when suddenly I was dragging my feet, walking unsteadily. I stopped, and I could see everything in front of me running away from me very quickly. I walked farther. I tried to stop, but I couldn't. I was propelled forward, staggered, and fell. It was another hypoglycemic attack, a replica of the previous incident.

Just at this time, another Malay security guard happened to pass by. He helped me to get up. I asked him to help me to open up the glucose container I had, and I consumed the glucose. The guard told me that he was under the impression that I was drunk. I cannot fault him because this is how my gait would be just before crashing, like a drunk person. I explained my condition to him and later thanked him.

Fig. 11 please also refer to page 117.

Another similar incident also took place. As usual, I went for a morning walk. On this day, I was walking nearer to my home at the entrance to the housing estate named Lian Garden. At one stage, I could feel that I was getting into a hypo state. This time, I did not want to take any risk. I could see that I was walking very unsteadily. Then I stopped near houses occupied by policemen. As this was in the morning, only the children and wives were in the houses. I walked with an unsteady gait to a house, and I asked a boy to call his mother to get a sweet drink. I could hear the boy calling his mother in the Malay language, describing me as *mabuk*, or drunk. When the lady came out, I managed to explain my condition to her. She mixed some coffee with sugar, and after consuming it, I felt better. This time, I did not risk taking a chance walking back, so I used my mobile to call my wife who had to get the help of my neighbor to come fetch me.

The two incidents where two individuals thought I was drunk well illustrate the symptoms resulting from hypoglycemia experienced during walks where excess energy had been used up. Because you are very unsteady, look blank, and have a peculiar stare, people unfamiliar with your condition will presume that you are drunk.

But there were also many instances of hypoglycemia symptoms experienced while driving with my wife. I would drive and apply the brakes suddenly. In one or two instances, I was not even able to recognize turns that were all too familiar to me. On seeing this, my wife would be alerted, and she would then open up the cover of the sweet drink that I keep in my car and pass it on to me. Then I would be fine.

I bring along a bottle of sweet drink, and other than a small container of glucose in my pocket, I keep two such containers in the glove compartment in the car. Whenever I travel long distances, I make sure I bring along another bottle of mixed cordial. This is a consequence of the bitter experiences I've encountered previously, such as those mentioned.

In my experiences while walking or exercising, I've found that a mixed and more diluted cordial drink is the quickest way to help with a low blood sugar level. Glucose in powder form is good, but glucose alone will take a long time to be absorbed into the bloodstream if it is not taken together with water. Second, the content of saliva will also not be of much help because, during exercise, one will tend to be dehydrated, and the mouth will be very dry and parched. I had already experienced this in the very bad attack I had in 1989.

In the latter part of 2009, again while going for my morning walk, I had a very bad attack of hypoglycemia. The reactions were all too similar to those mentioned previously. On this day, I was walking along a road not frequented by vehicles. No one else was to be seen at the time.

I knew I was getting into a bad situation. I was hoping that someone young and strong would be there to hold me and at least break my fall. But this was not to be. I staggered, and while falling, I hit my forehead on a stone.

I had some bruises but fortunately not serious ones. As usual, after the fall, I was up and about and walked back to my eldest sister's house, about a ten-minute walk away.

CHAPTER 30

A Sliding Fall

In the month of July 2010, as usual, after skimming through the newspapers, I read spiritual books in the living room. At that particular time as well, my wife was reading the newspaper. The time was about ten in the morning.

As I was reading, I found I was straining to read the same lines over and over again. It was as though I was trying to figure out words and sentences. I became cross-eyed trying to decipher letters and words. This continued for quite some time.

By now, my wife, upon noticing my face and staring eyes, told me to take the sweet drink that was in the fridge. So I walked to the kitchen. But when I came to the kitchen, I was just standing around, not knowing what to do. I was in a terrible hypoglycemic state. Realizing the lack of positive response after her calls, she rushed to the kitchen.

My condition turned from bad to worse. I could hardly balance. There was nothing to hold on to in the kitchen. My wife was in a dilemma because, on one hand, she had to think of my already-bad state. On the other hand, she had to mix the glucose and cordial drink. At that very moment, I was about to fall and so as a drowning man would, I grabbed the hand of my feather weight wife and consequently she fell too.

I felt very aggrieved on seeing her fall. But in no way could I help even though I was solely responsible for whatever had taken place. In the meantime, I staggered to the wall, a few inches from the refrigerator just to make the wall a support for my back to break the fall.

Just after I had touched the wall, I crashed to the ground, the full weight of seventy-four kilos following me. My first thought was that I had fractured my spine. The first thing I did was pinch both my legs, my toes, and my skin to see if I had sensations. Then I moved my toes and legs to ensure nothing untoward had taken place. After the fall, as usual, the hypo symptoms disappeared. I took the cordial mixed by my wife, and I was also happy to see her all right.

After this, both of us went to the Mawar Hospital nearby to consult the orthopedic specialist, Mr. Naveed. He examined both my legs thoroughly and then sent me for an X-ray for the lower portion of my back. Fortunately, the results showed no damage.

CHAPTER 31

An Unusually Long Bath

Again, in 2010, being in a hypo state but unaware of it, I went to my washroom to have my shower. It was about three thirty in the afternoon. I must have been in the washroom for a long time. Knowing something must have gone wrong, my wife called to see if everything were all right. The shower was on, and my answers were vague

My wife told me to unlock the door, but I could not. I was grasping the showerhead for balance and hit the plastic tub of water and then the wall, all this as a consequence of not being able to keep my balance and stand up.

When my wife heard the commotion within, she kicked the door, which fortunately was made of plastic. The plastic latch broke. When my wife came in, I was lying on the floor with the shower on.

She at once gave me some cordial, and I recovered very soon. I had my bath and resumed my normal chores.

OSTEOPOROSIS OF RIGHT KNEE

From my days as a young boy, through my youth, and as an adult, I was not physically inactive. I used to jog regularly on hard surfaces, and probably this together with my age may have resulted in damage to my right knee. I was getting severe pain around my right knee, especially when I went for walks.

I had no choice but to consult Mr. Naveed, the orthopedic surgeon, who, after doing X-rays and physical examinations, injected the area around my right knee three times with hyaluronic acid gel. This was a temporary relief and was supposed to last for about eight months. I was advised not to walk uphill but instead to walk on level ground.

However, after the injection, as I felt better than normal, I did not heed the doctor's advice and continued to walk as I normally would. After six months, the pain became very severe, a consequence of bone knocking bone. After consulting Mr. Naveed again, on December 27, 2011, he did an arthroscopy on my right knee. In the course of the surgery, on a screen he showed me that my lower knee bone was smooth, meaning that there was no cushioning. He also told me that he had made four holes in the bone called a fracture so these would somewhat form a healing just as any other fracture would.

For some months after the scope was performed, I had to adjust to the way I sat. Sitting for a long time in my normal position would cause pain and still does. Wearing a knee guard does help. However, while sitting at home to read or watch television, I often have to rest my right leg on a puff. Driving for long distances is also a problem. Still today, I cannot do brisk walks. However, the consolation is that I can at least walk, albeit slowly, for about an hour or so. I was advised that, if the knee were painful, I was to sit for at least five minutes. This does help.

CHAPTER 32

Worst Fall Ever

On December 1, 2012, I had the worst fall ever. That morning when I tested my blood sugar level, the reading was 2.4 mml. The advice on the pamphlet that came with the insulin was that, if the pre-breakfast reading were less than 4.4 mml, the insulin dose of thirty units was to be reduced by two units. But I didn't reduce it. To make matters worse, that was also the day I did my morning walks. I injected myself with the thirty units of insulin and took in more food for breakfast. The problem is that insulin acts within a half hour, whereas food that is consumed takes a longer time to be absorbed into the bloodstream.

After I had completed about fifty-two minutes of walking, I found that I was slowing down for no apparent reason. Although I do not walk as briskly as I used to because of the knee problem, I found myself dragging my feet and walking with an unsteady gait. Suspecting that I was in for a hypo attack, I stopped to do my usual test—that is, looking at the road, trees, and objects ahead of me. Sure enough, I could see the road and trees in front moving quickly away from me.

I stopped to take the glucose powder that I always carry in my pocket. But, as my mouth was very parched, consuming glucose alone without water would not bring the immediate effect that one would hope for. I even put some glucose under my tongue where the area was wet.

Being obstinate, I made up my mind that I should complete the balance of the eight-minute walk—that is, to complete an hour. If only I had walked up to my car, which was parked about eighty meters away, the incident I am about to relate would not have happened. In my car, I had a bottle of cordial, and consuming this would have given me instant relief.

After consuming the glucose, I felt a little better, so I continued walking up and down the road near the main office of the Health Department, the same area where I had been jogging and then walking since the 1980s.

But at about eight fifty-two in the morning, my hypo condition turned worse. I was desperately looking around for help, but as it was a weekend, not a soul was to be seen. There was a guard at the department, but she was in her guardhouse. I desperately needed someone to support me or put me down on the ground. From previous experiences, I knew I was about to crash-land. I walked to a lamppost, hoping to hold it tight, but this was not to be. Again, as if by an unknown force, I was propelled forward. I tried to use the thick rattan cane I used as a walking stick to support and break the fall, but it was of no use. I crashed facedown, hitting my nose and damaging my spectacles.

When I got up, I saw many drops of blood dripping on a white plastic sheet that was on the ground. I wiped the blood on my T-shirt and later used my handkerchief to clean the blood on my nose. As usual, after the heavy fall, I came back to my normal self. I took out the mobile phone from my pocket and snapped a few photos of my injuries at the place of the incident.

Fig. 12. Plastic sheet at scene of fall into Blood stain on plastic
sheet, please also refer to Figs. 13 & 14, pages 118, 119.

Later, I walked up to the guardroom at the Health Office to
ask the female guard to get me some water so I could take it with
the glucose. The bleeding from my nose stopped, but there were
bruises on both my elbows. The pain on the bridge of my nose
continued for about two weeks. At the time of the fall, I tried to
avoid landing on my right knee, which had been operated on about
a year before.

Even at this state of a hypoglycemic attack, my awareness was
there, but as for physical movements, I was totally unable to do
anything. In all the hypoglycemic incidents mentioned previously, I
knew very well the condition I was in, but I just could not keep my
body still. It was as though some force from within was pushing me
with all its might forward at a fast pace.

However, after the fall, having wiped off all the blood, I walked back to the car, took some more cordial, and then returned home, a seven-minute drive away. This was the first time that I had fallen after the use of a new type of insulin since May 2012.

In May 2012, when I went for my quarterly yearly checkup at the Tuanku Jaafar Hospital, the physician who was attending to me, Dr. Singham, advised me to use the Novo FlexPen. This pen is prefilled with insulin, and the patient only has to attach a disposable needle and remove it after use. The pen is like an ink cartridge, which is disposed of after use.

This pen actually has a mixed component of fast-acting and slow-acting insulin in one tube, whereas formerly I used to inject myself twice, once with the fast-acting Actrapid and then the slow-acting Monotard. So now, instead of injecting myself twice in the mornings and twice in the evenings, I only had to inject myself twice a day, once in the morning and then again in the evening. Earlier, when I had asked Dr. Thayaparan about the older version of this insulin called Mixtard, he told me that, in my case, it was not possible, as my dose was high, and they did not have such calibrations in Mixtard.

This Novo FlexPen was actually a great relief for me. For one, I spent much less time in the process of injecting. Each time I used to inject, I had to draw the insulin from one vial and then inject. And immediately after that, I had to take the other syringe, draw insulin again from the other vial, and finally put these in their respective places. But now, it was so very easy. At long last, both the fast-acting and slow-acting insulin were mixed together and sealed in a pen. I just had to shake or roll the pen in my palm after removing the cover to get the contents mixed properly. Then I just had to attach the separately purchased needle and inject myself. This is so simple and almost painless. Once again, I would like readers to make a comparison of the sizes of needles and syringes from 1957 till now (Figs 5-7) for a self explanatory explanation of improvements in syringes and needles.

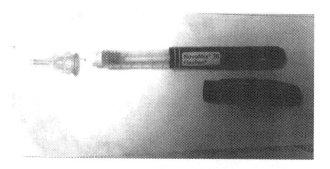

Please see page 113 (3)

I was advised to inject myself with thirty units in the morning and thirty units in the evening. Although the prescribed dose was thirty units in the mornings and thirty units in the evenings, I had to either increase or decrease the dosage in conformity with the results from the glucometer tests. I did not follow this on December 1.

I shall explain the differences between the insulins of Actrapid, Monotard, and Humulin R and Humulin N. In actual fact, the difference is only in the brands. The dosage need not be adjusted if a switch is made from one to another. The only difference is in the pen where both brands had their own versions.

As for the Novo FlexPen, I find that it causes rapid fluctuation in blood sugar levels. One morning when I tested my blood sugar, the reading on the glucometer was 2.3 mml. This is considered low. I took some sweet drink and, I think, a biscuit.

When I tested my blood sugar level again after two and a half hours, the meter read 10.1 mml. Even though this is this fluctuation, look at what happened to me on December 1. Insulin under any name is insulin. So, be careful. That is my advice.

A WAKE-UP CALL

Every morning, I set my alarm to ring at about four ten to do my ablutions before prayers. If I did not respond after the alarm had rung, my wife would call me to see if I were responding. Often when I did not respond, she would get up to mix some cordial and use a spoon to put it into my mouth, sometimes without success.

There was one instance when she heard me making some very strange sounds about two in the morning. When there was no response, she rushed to the kitchen and mixed cordial and glucose. She had to keep forcing glucose powder and cordial into my mouth. She told me that I spat out everything. Only at about five was I aware of what was happening. She was nearly in tears and told me that she was on the verge of calling for an ambulance. The whole pillow, along with the bedsheet, was wet with the spilled cordial.

When I recovered, I first asked my wife for the time. I was very disciplined about getting up early to do my ablutions before prayers. Because it was five, I got up and then had my shower after brushing my teeth. However, I was not able to do my meditation as the three hours or more in a hypoglycemic condition had taken a toll on my system.

CHAPTER 33

Hypoglycemic Symptoms and Attacks in India

In 1998, I, together with Mr. Rajoo, a lawyer with whom I was working in the firm by the name of Rajoo and Co., decided to go on a tour to India. We were centered at Madras (now Tamil Nadu) and visited several other places. Rajoo knew of my diabetic condition and off and on used to inquire about my condition.

One morning while asleep, I suddenly started mentioning the name of a well-known lawyer who has since passed on. When Mr. Rajoo heard me, he told me, "Siva, you are in India." He asked me if I were all right. Dazed, I got up but managed to drink some sweet drinks that were in the hotel fridge.

I am an initiated devotee of the Swami Bhoomananda Tirtha of the state of Kerala in India. In December 2005, I went to the ashram with my cousin Paramanathan; his wife, Vasantha; and another devotee, Devi. Devotees from Malaysia often visit the ashram to imbibe spiritual knowledge by listening to talks by the swami, our guru.

In the ashram too, I had a very bad hypoglycemic attack on December 21. According to my cousin, who was sleeping in the same room, at about three or three thirty, I was making funny sounds, and on examination, he found I was frothing very badly. The ashram was informed, and a devotee and inmate named

Ramaswamy then made the necessary arrangements for me to be taken to Elite Medical Hospital. Paramanathan and Ramaswamy stayed with me until I recovered after the administration of glucose drips. Neither Ramaswamy nor my cousin, in whose house I stayed in 1958, had ever seen such an episode. I felt shattered because I had put so many people, especially Ramaswamy, who was and even now busy with lots of work at the ashram, through difficulty caused by my attack. I felt terribly bad and guilty as I had put many people into unnecessary concern and difficulty. When I had recovered, my cousin returned to the ashram, and after some time, he returned to take me back to the ashram.

In 2010, I once again felt like going to the ashram together with another devotee, Sivagnanam (Siva). Before the advent of this trip, I asked my guru if I could come to the ashram for a week's stay. My guru advised me against it. I was very disheartened. I told him that I would take all the necessary precautions to avoid a repetition of the 2005 incident. As I was intent on going, he finally acceded.

Siva and I reached the ashram on December 13. Two other devotees from Malaysia, Unni Krishnan and his wife, Rema Menon, were already at the ashram. In the evenings, many devotees, including myself, Siva, and Unnikrishnan, used to go for walks. Although I used to exercise regularly, these two men were too fast for me. However, every day at the ashram, we would walk for about an hour through the paddy fields, roads with greenery beside them, houses, and so on. It was very enjoyable, especially the walks through the paddy fields where we used to see ducks, goats, and cows grazing.

On December 15, both Unnikrishnan and Siva had personal matters to attend to. As was my habit, I wanted to exercise. I did not go on the normal routes I took with the two other devotees, as I was not familiar with the place and surroundings. So I climbed a steep hill with many steps. On the topmost was situated the Pandava Giri Hills and a temple. These were just situated behind and atop the ashram. From the hill, if you look out, you have a beautiful sight of the paddy fields along which we used to walk.

After reaching the top of this temple, I walked down a road by which people from the villages or town could come to the temple. I walked down the road, which was very steeply inclined, and then walked up again. Then I returned to the ashram by walking down the steps again.

I was really perspiring. Never during the walks in the ashram had I sweated as much as I did on December 15. I felt very elated, alert, and fresh but tired. That very night, all the ashramites (devotees) had dinner as usual. All of us were served with something that looked like rice, white in color. I took more, as I knew that I had burned up a lot of calories. Only later did Ramaswamy tell me that it was actually made from the inner layers of the banana tree trunk. It was not rice—therefore, not starch but fiber. Eating fiber can result in low blood sugar, and this is what resulted the following morning.

According to Siva, at about three in the morning on December 16, he heard me making very strange noises. When he got up to wake me up, there was no response. He called Unnikrishan, who was in another room, and both knew my condition and the steps to take. They tried to revive me, but alas, there was no response. They gave me—or rather tried to give me—glucose powder together with cordial drink, which I had put on the table, but failed. My guru was informed, and he came to my room. I was told he pinched me, but I did not respond.

Then an ambulance was called, and once again, I was taken to Elite Medical Hospital, as was the case in 2005. Siva, Unnikrishnan, and Ramaswamy, who also accompanied me to the hospital in 2005, accompanied me to the hospital on December 16, 2010.

When I recovered, I found myself surrounded by the above-mentioned, lying on a bed with drips on my hand. There, in front of me, I saw a young, very pleasant doctor, Dr. Priya Darshini. When she asked me about the dosage and type of insulin I was taking, with clarity, I was able to tell the exact dosage of the Actrapid and Monotard insulin I was then injecting myself with.

She also inquired about the other medications and drugs I was taking.

After a short duration, I asked to be discharged, but I was told they had to keep me under observation in the event that I went into another hypo attack. However, a short while later, I was discharged and sent back, still with the drips attached.

I returned to my room and had to lie down with the drips on my hand. Later, Ramaswamy, who had some experience and medical knowledge, removed the drip and covered the needle entry point with gauze and plaster.

After some time, this "roly-poly doll" brushed his teeth, had his bath, and injected the morning insulin dose. Later, I went to have my breakfast, which was set aside for me. All the other devotees were attending to talks by guru and two others, a swami and a nun.

Later that same morning, at the second session of prayers and satsang (gathering of like-minded devotees), my guru asked me how I was. For the first time, I told him the whole history, and when I was diagnosed with diabetes in 1957, the term used was "juvenile" diabetes. Now it is type 1. I also related to him why the incident could have happened, the instance of going up and down the hill and then up the hill again, and the dinner where the fiber had possibly reduced my blood sugar level.

There were also other reasons that could have brought about this attack in the year 2005 herein at the ashram. The ashram covers a large area, so the devotees have to walk from one place to another to hear talks, attend prayers, have food, and then walk back to the respective rooms away from the ashram itself. So I would have used up a lot of energy on a daily basis during the stay at the ashram.

After this particular incident, Siva and Unrikrishnan constantly checked on me, reminding me to check my sugar level before going to bed and even at other times. For both of them, it was a first-time experience of a diabetic going into a very bad hypoglycemic attack.

One day after the hypo attack in the ashram, as I passed my guru, he remarked that, though I had been a juvenile diabetic, I did not portray myself as one. For most people, diabetes was like a death sentence. But today with all the medical knowledge and medication available, diabetes can be easily controlled, and anyone can lead a good life, provided he controls sugar intake, does regular exercise, and, of course, takes the prescribed medication regularly.

Whenever I have a teleconversation with my guru, along with when he comes down every year in the month of August to deliver spiritual talks in various towns and Kuala Lumpur, he would inquire about my health.

ANOTHER POSSIBLE INCIDENCE OF HYPO ATTACK AVOIDED

On May 11, 2013, as usual when I tested my blood sugar at about four twenty before I went upstairs for my morning prayers, the reading was 8.9 mml. For me, this was high. After about an hour or so, I came down, injected myself with thirty units of Novo FlexPen insulin, and then had my breakfast. After that, I changed into my shorts and T-shirt to go out for my morning walk. But then I felt that something was not in order. I started feeling lazy, taking a long time to do something that would only take a few minutes under normal circumstances. I did not feel good. Just as I was about to go out, I was wobbly as I walked. I never suspected that I was already in hypo because of the high reading in the morning.

To avoid another recurrence of the many attacks I had in my walks, I decided to do another blood sugar test. It was 2.2 mml. My wife immediately mixed some cordial drink, which I took. I decided not to go out for the walk. Instead, I did cycling on the stationary bicycle for about an hour. I was indeed grateful that the hypo symptom showed up before I left the house. This is another example of what is meant by brittle diabetes. One moment, the reading may be high; at another moment, it can be very low or vice versa.

Ever since I was introduced to the Novo FlexPen insulin in mid-2012, the person made happiest by this has been my wife. Now at least she sleeps soundly when the alarm goes off at four ten. When I was on Actrapid/Monotard insulin, very often I had to be attended to when I failed to wake up. I have already mentioned numerous incidents that occurred when I was on the older versions of insulin. Now with this Novo FlexPen, I have had only one very bad experience, on December 1, 2012, as related. The other incidents above did not bring about undue stress on any of us.

On the plus side, this Novo FlexPen insulin, insofar as I am concerned, does not result in aggressive actions, unlike the other insulin I was using. It is mild, and even if the hypoglycemic symptoms persist, I am able to at least resort to quick reactions.

On the minus side, I find that I am unable to consume anything extra even if I want to. Unlike the older version of insulin, if any extra food, even a little bit extra, is consumed, my blood sugar level shoots up. Formerly, whenever I tested my blood sugar in the evenings at about four o'clock, the average reading was always at about 4.0 mml. More often than not, it was about 3.5 mml or so. But these days, the average reading is about 6.4 mml or more. A few times, the readings went to up 11.3 mml and once even to 13.4 mml, all these in spite of the fact that I skip lunch. I feel lucky that I do not get into frequent hypoglycemic attacks.

CHAPTER 34

Further Advice From My Experience

This year, 2013, it will be about fifty-six years since I was diagnosed as a juvenile diabetic. Now although I have far passed the stage of a juvenile, I am still a type 1 diabetic resorting to daily doses of insulin. Albeit a retiree, I make sure that I keep myself fit either by going for walks or riding my stationary bicycle. I do this at least three or four times a week. As an advice to all diabetics, whether type 1 or type 2, I do never neglect to take the medication or insulin prescribed. From my experience, I know that, if I ever delayed the insulin intake by even a few hours, my blood sugar level would go up in the event that I consumed any food or drink.

For a type 1 diabetic, the affected should use good discrimination and awareness to monitor his glucose level. These days, there are so many glucose-monitoring machines and test strips. Whenever I test my blood sugar level, my memory suddenly rushes back to the days when I had to use up a lot of time with the older method.

My other advice to those who lead active lives or are involved in physical activities is for them to consider adjusting their dosage. This is best done with the advice of their physicians, but from my experience, insofar as this is concerned, we are the best doctors. Doctors and instructions in the manual can only be specific up to a certain point, but from personal experience, we alone know about the body and its symptoms best.

As a retiree, I am not physically active. But when I go for my morning walks, I have to ensure that I eat more than my normal breakfast to avoid a hypoglycemic attack. Even this may not be sufficient if, for instance, my morning blood sugar level is low. The many instances of falls that I have related previously are proof of this. It is indeed very difficult to specifically state what is the best dosage or adjustment to dosage because every individual is different physically, metabolically, and mentally. Only through experience can this be ascertained.

While exercising, especially when jogging or briskly walking, if you become unsteady or start dragging your feet, just stand still and look straight ahead at the ground in front of you.

If you see the road, trees, or grass ahead of you rushing backward, you are most likely already in a hypoglycemic condition. From my experience, I find that the lower the blood sugar level, the faster everything recedes. Sometimes when I've stood on one spot, I could see all the things in front of me moving very swiftly. If my blood sugar level is not very low, the receding is very slow. So, at this stage, some sweet drink or glucose should be taken, preferably with water.

Until December 1, 2012, I only carried two plastic containers of glucose but no water. I used to keep a bottle of cordial in the car. The consequence of this was all the incidents of hypoglycemic experiences reported herein. Since my attack on December 1, I've had a few warnings of impending attacks, but I was able to avert any untoward attack by taking glucose powder with the cordial drink I carried in my pocket. But before consuming these, I used to do the usual tests to see if I was going into a hypoglycemic state.

As further advice and perhaps words of caution to newly diagnosed diabetics on medication, I would like to mention that exercise is very necessary for a diabetic. Exercise may be done in any form, depending of course on your age, mental strength, and determination. When I was much younger, I used jog a lot and play games like badminton. But now at the age of sixty-seven and with osteoarthritis in my right knee, I can only do slow walks, so I make it a point to walk for at least one hour. If I do not go out for my walks, I cycle on my stationary bicycle for an hour. Thankfully, this discipline has been with me since I was young and more so after the physicians advised me of the importance of exercise.

With exercise, those who are on medication, especially on insulin, have to be cautious about getting into hypoglycemic conditions. Whenever we exercise, we burn up calories. Of course, the amount of calories burned depends on the kind of exercise one is performing. While in open space, you may look out for symptoms of hypoglycemia I have mentioned previously. But for indoors activities, the symptoms will be very different.

Once while I was on my stationary bicycle, I didn't realize I was already in hypo, but I continued cycling. Suddenly, I lost my balance, missed the pedals, and nearly fell off my bicycle. Another time, I was on a treadmill in my home. I had already been on the machine for about forty-five minutes and was jogging at a good pace. Suddenly, I felt that I was losing my balance, and I lost my footing and fell flat on the treadmill. Fortunately, I escaped injury. I'm specifically mentioning this because symptoms of hypoglycemia may vary depending on the duration that a person has been afflicted with diabetes.

For me, even with a low reading, I am unable to recognize my symptoms unless a person who is familiar with my condition warns me. If you exercise with others, let them know about your diabetic condition, the type of medication you are on, and what they should possibly do in the event of a hypoglycemic attack. Better still, for those unfamiliar with the pre-hypo symptoms, advise them on what to look for while you are exercising together.

The advice I would give again is to always carry a small plastic bottle containing diluted syrup and glucose. In or before a hypoglycemic attack, a combination of both is the best remedy. In fact, this advice came to my aid on June 1, 2013. It was a Saturday, a day when I usually go for walks.

In the morning when I did my blood sugar test, the reading was 2.2 mml (very low). In spite of the fact that it was so low, I got up on my own when the alarm rang at four ten, did the test, and immediately took some cordial, together with low sugar soya bean drink. I also ate some peanuts. Then I went to have my bath and later did my prayers.

Normally, as mentioned earlier, when I'm on hypo, work that could normally be done in a short time drags on for a much longer period. This is what happened on June 1. I did everything I had to do as usual and then had my breakfast at about six fifty, and I repeated the same mistake I made on December 1, 2012. Instead of reducing my dosage by two units, I injected myself with the normal dosage. Then I started on my walk. After about a half hour of walking, at about eight ten, I became unsteady. I did my usual tests. Things seemed normal, yet I felt very uneasy. I continued my walk. Just as I was near the army camp, I once again did the usual vision test, and then I could see the road in front of me and trees beside me receding slowly.

I felt it was too early for me to take any sweet stuff, so I kept walking. This time, after walking for about 150 meters, I realized I was in a fix. I quickly took out my glucose container, took a little bit of glucose, and also took a bit of cordial I had in my pocket. This helped a little. I continued walking. But after a short distance, I became very unsteady again. I stood still to check my vision. This time, sure enough, all the objects in front of me, including the road, were running away. I knew I was in for another attack. Immediately, I emptied more of the glucose and consumed all of the cordial drink I had. Then I waited. Instantly I felt as though a lot of pressure had been relieved from my system. I felt normal, walked back to my car, and topped off the plastic container with cordial I had in my car.

Later, I completed my hour of walking. This time, having learned that I needed to carry fluids after the December 1 incident, the cordial drink I took together with the glucose saved me. Glucose powder alone would have resulted in another great fall.

In repetition, it may be stated that while one is actively exercising, specially so if he has been afflicted with this condition for a number of years, that person may not even realize that he is going into a hypoglycaemic state. He may want to complete his walk, jog, or, for that matter, any other form of calorie-burning activity in the time frame and manner he had planned for that particular day. Please be reminded that herein lies the danger.

If the early symptoms are overlooked or not acted upon and the person continues to exercise, the oxygen supply to the brain especially and the body in general depletes due to lack of glucose in the bloodstream. During this period of time, he, though aware of this dangerous situation, may not be in a position to inform people or ask for help, let alone do anything to address the symptoms on his own. He will not be in a position to think coherently, and in this state, he is bound to crash-land. This is while exercising. Can you imagine if this happened while handling a vehicle?

I write very confidently because I have experienced all these symptoms over the years. All these incidents I describe have actually taken place in my case. I do not relay these stories to cause apprehension in anyone; however, I always encourage diabetics to do regular exercise in any form in order to burn calories and help in overall health, if, while exercising, they take care to monitor their blood sugar levels.

I can confidently attest that exercise is a must for diabetics, having been a type 1 diabetic for fifty-six years (1957-2013) with insulin injections twice or sometimes more times daily.

The second must—and I should say an even more important one—is to keep a strict watch on diet. To this day, a dietician has never advised me. In 1957, there were no dieticians in the hospitals. Today, they have them, but doctors never asked me to see one. After reading every quarterly blood test, they've felt that I have good control over my blood sugar, along with cholesterol and blood pressure, though these are with medications as advised by Dr. Thayaparan.

When I was diagnosed with diabetes in 1957, first doctors and then nurses told me not to consume rice, apples, or anything sweet. Somehow I managed to maintain good diet control, though at times I was careless. These days, if either my wife or I buy packaged foods or drinks, we read the labels for calorie content; these can be misleading at times.

But at least one can know about the highest and lowest calorie intake as per 100 milliliters. In this way, for example, if I like a drink a lot, I can get a taste of it, but I need to consume much less than what a nondiabetic can drink or eat. I do not have to forbid myself from eating any kind of food, but I have to be intelligent about it and consume very little if the calorie content is high and consume more if the calorie content is low. This is living smartly and wisely.

Sometimes when I really love a particular food, I eat to my satisfaction. But that has conditions attached. First, I skip a meal to compensate. Second, as I am a brittle diabetic, I do a blood sugar test, and if I find the sugar level has gone up, I administer myself with a few extra units of fast-acting insulin. This is to prevent my blood sugar level from swinging. Sad to say, I have come across many people who are confirmed diabetics, either type 1 or type 2, who curse and swear at the disease, not helping themselves in any way.

I used to attend wedding functions where I saw these diabetics indulge or gorge themselves, with the whole rationale of diet just disregarded. Not only that, especially at Hindu weddings, a last dish called *paya sam* in Tamil—vermicillin mixed with cashew nuts, raisins, and sometimes other ingredients—is served. This dish, after water is added, is sweetened with lots of brown or white sugar. So consuming this dessert is actually like drinking thick sugar. On one hand, people seem to complain about diabetes. On the other hand, greed or lack of good control is their bane.

Often I am shocked by the quantity of food on diabetic people's plates. I do not mean to complain about the amount they eat or the foods they enjoy, but I get disgusted that these are the very same people who profess that they are very careful with their diet when they seek my advice, knowing I have been a longtime diabetic.

At the present, nearly all hospitals, both public and private, have counsellors to advise both prediabetic and confirmed diabetic patients. These patients are then referred to dieticians who give them pamphlets that clearly state the quantity of food that is to be taken at any one time. Of course, foods with high sugar content should either be totally omitted, or if taken, they should be consumed in very small proportions.

From my own experience, in the event I crave a particular food that is restricted for a diabetic, I eat only a small portion of it. For example, in my town, if I buy a small ice cream cone, I would usually eat just the cone together with a little ice cream. My wife will eat the rest of it. But this usually happens once or twice a year at most.

When I had been confirmed as a diabetic in 1957, my mother once prepared a cup of milo without sugar and offered it to me to drink; my mother felt sympathy and perhaps thought just one drink would do no harm. But I declined it for the simple reason that milo is sweet, or tastes sweet anyway. As milo tasted sweet and doctors had cautioned me against consuming sweet edibles and drinks, I followed their advice and hence refused the milo drink.

CHAPTER 35

A Meal Too Much

On May 19, 2005, I underwent a cataract operation on my left eye at the Tuanku Jaafar General Hospital in my hometown of Seremban. It was a day-care surgery—that is, after the operation, patients rest at the wards and are later discharged.

As per instructions, I was admitted at six thirty in the morning. After admission, the nurses test all eye surgery patients for their blood sugar and blood pressure. My readings were normal.

At about noon, I could sense that I was going into a hypoglycemic condition. I related this to my wife, who was also with me. She then informed the staff nurse. Sure enough, when my blood was tested, it read 1.5 mml, a very low level. My wife, as usual, brought along some fiber biscuits and the usual mixed cordial drink. Knowing my condition that if I consumed a lot of these out of apprehension or fear my blood sugar level would rise, perhaps even to double figures, as per my "brittle" condition, I consumed just two pieces of biscuits and a little cordial drink.

At lunchtime, each patient was given a tray with rice, vegetables, and chicken in curry form. I know through my experience that rice can be a culprit. The head of the eye department Dr Bethyl Livingstone had specific instructions to her staff that patients who were diabetic and whose sugar level readings were high would not be operated upon. All patients are aware of this because, prior to the surgery, all patients must undergo blood sugar and blood pressure tests. For blood sugar, it was the usual HbA1c tests. These tests show the sugar control for the previous three to four months.

Opposite me were two other patients waiting for their turn to be operated upon, one directly and the other behind the other divide. The patient directly opposite me was supposed to be operated on first. But this did not occur. Both the above mentioned were also diabetics. When lunch was served, I observed that these two patients ate up most or all of the food served. When I noticed this, at first I thought perhaps their conditions were not as severe as mine, but I told my wife that both these people were asking for trouble. I was very right.

Just before surgery for the patient opposite me, his blood sugar was tested. Then the other patient's sugar level was also tested. Both their readings were very high, and consequently, they were asked to return home and undergo the whole process again; they could not be operated on at this time. The patient opposite me made a huge fuss, but he failed to understand that, first, it was for his own good. Second, all the prerequisites were within his knowledge. This applied to every patient in this clinic.

I was lucky because I had a chance to be operated upon earlier. My blood sugar level was tested, and it read 5 mml. It was good. I was then wheeled in and operated on. Had I been carefree in consuming too much food, knowing that my sugar level was very low, I would have had the same results as the patients opposite me, needing to go through the whole rigmarole of doing all the presurgery tests. I would have to come back for the eye surgery, perhaps on a much later date, due to the number of patients on the waiting list. Knowing the nature of brittle diabetes, I skipped the lunch that was served. I would like to stress again that a diabetic is the best judge of his diabetic condition. As such, he should adapt and live intelligently and, hence, healthily.

I am offering my advice to diabetics and nondiabetics to lead smart lives. By this, I mean, when purchasing edible items, you should read the labels to evaluate the calorie/kilojoule content and, knowing this, to adjust the total amount consumed.

If diabetes is not well controlled over a period of time, it can lead to collateral damage to the kidneys and eyes. Furthermore, if a person sustains cuts or even scratches and if these are untreated, it may lead to amputation of the affected part or more of it. These days, we read and see a lot about these in the media.

CHAPTER 36

A Lesson Learnt

When I was admitted to the Tuanku Jaafar General Hospital in 1973 for my tonsils operation, a customs officer was in the same room in the ward. His leg was amputated right up to the knee. When I inquired from him as to the cause, he told me that, while he was in his garden, a glass piece had cut his toe. He did not seek treatment but just washed the cut and applied some medication. But unknown to him, he was a latent diabetic. Only when gangrene set in did he see a doctor, but as it was already too late, the infected half of the leg had to be amputated.

Although diabetes is a life-endangering disease if not intelligently managed, any diabetic can lead a near-normal life as long as he heeds the advice of medical practitioners and dieticians.

I shall herein mention an incident where I was careless with my food intake. From February 27, 2013, I had been eating a lot of tidbits, more or less reveling in a binge. I am an eater of peanuts, both fried and roasted. On my request, my wife would buy peanuts, a number of small packets, and also some stuff for herself. I ate a lot of these. Not surprisingly, my sugar level readings rose. From a normal average reading of between 5.0 and 6.0 mml, the readings shot up to between 9.0 and 11.0 and once even went up to 13.4 mml. For me, one who was always very strict about sugar level control, this created a concern.

Although I stopped the binge after a few days upon realizing my folly, my blood sugar level did not record a normal reading. It was still on the high side, so I became concerned. I reflected on 1970, when I had Koch's infection. I compared my bodily conditions from 1970 and now. In 1970, when I had the infection, I started losing weight. But now I wasn't losing weight. The only similarity in my conditions was the urine sugar level readings then and the blood sugar level readings now, both of which were high.

Stillconcerned about my high blood sugar level, I rang up my niece, Dr. Dakshineswari, a medical officer in the government service. She is actually the daughter of my sister Dr. Rajeswari and her husband, Dr. Asohandran. She, in turn, told me that she would give me a form with which to record the blood sugar readings four times a day, and I could show this record to my physician after making an appointment.

I was still not happy. I put on my thinking cap. Only then did I realize that the cause of my high blood sugar readings could be my increase in weight after the crazy binge episode. I have a tendency to put on body mass very quickly. To put the matter to rest, I decided to weigh myself. Sure enough, I had put on three kilos. For me, extra kilos means a higher sugar level.

Having located the source of my high sugar level, I had to revert to my usual diet without consuming extra food or tidbits unless, of course, I had to resort to these when my sugar level dipped very low. This discipline worked. When I tested my blood sugar on February 28, 2013, at about four in the afternoon, the reading was 3.1 mml. I mention these particularly to let diabetics and nondiabetics know that control of the kind of food consumed should be of utmost importance.

Here is another instance of fluctuation in my blood sugar levels. After all the concerns as related in chapter 36 above on February 28 2013 , I injected myself with the usual morning dosage of thirty units f Novo Flex Pen insulin. At about noon on the same day, I felt that I was low on sugar. When I tested my blood sugar, the reading was 3.1 mml. To me, this was normal. Although I knew that my sugar level would decrease as time passed by, I did not consume anything after all the anxiety the previous week.

But there was also another reason why I didn't consuming anything. A few days earlier, feeling very uneasy, I, as usual, did the blood sugar test to clear all my doubts. It was about noon. My guess was right, as the reading was a very low 1.8 mml. To avoid a hypoglycemic attack, I drank half the amount of a fifty-milliliter chrysanthemum tea with less sugar. Had I only stopped and waited for some time, this amount would have been perfect. But the problem with my condition is that, whenever my blood sugar is low and if I happen to take some sweet drink, I feel an immediate drop in my sugar level. This feeling at once triggers me into thinking that my condition is getting worse, and consequently, I pump in more sweet stuff, which is not necessary. This has happened not once but many times.

Such being the case, I drank a can of root beer that my wife had bought for herself and kept in the fridge. As expected, at about three thirty, when I tested my blood sugar level once more, the reading was a shocking 22.4 mml. It was sort of a record for my so-called strict sugar level control. So here again is another instance of what brittle diabetes means, from 1.8 mml at about noon to 22.4 mml at three thirty, a time span of about three and a half hours.

This is another incident I have deliberately mentioned to advise and maybe even warn that all bottled, canned, and packet drinks without reduced sugar content are extremely detrimental not only to diabetics but to nondiabetics as well. For nondiabetics, consuming all these sweet drinks, in my view, causes the pancreas to overwork, and this may later result in a person becoming a diabetic. I have read about these in magazines.

Following the above-mentioned episodes, I sent an SMS to my niece, Dr. Dakshineswari, which read as follows: "Back 2 normal. Reason, careless with diet! Lesson 4 yr Patients!" I had earlier contacted my niece about my sudden surge in blood sugar levels. So I had to reply, stating that the matter was settled. As for the mention of "Lesson 4 yr Patients," I messaged this so she could advise her patients who were very careless with their food.

During the course of conversation with her, she would frequently relate to me that most patients just do not heed her advice on food intake. Very often, she stated the blood sugar readings were extremely high. Many were initially diagnosed as type 2 diabetics, but because of their indifferent attitude to advice given by doctors and other medical staff, they had to graduate to type 2 diabetics on insulin.

On one hand, it is difficult to fault them because most are from a rural background, and often there is a mind-set in most of them that cannot be altered. Although today ignorance is not an excuse because of so much publicity via all the media, old habits seem to be embedded in many of them.

Many of the folks, both rural and urban, are fond of drinking tea or coffee with condensed milk. I have personally seen people asking for more condensed milk to be added. These are habits people have inculcated from their parents and grandparents, but many seem to forget that their parents—or rather great-grandparents—did a lot of physical activities. There were no vehicles; rather, bicycles were used. This is not so today, so lifestyle too has to change. But can this be done? It can be if only patients have patience to listen and follow attentively whatever advice has been given.

Many folks also love to eat traditional delicacies that are extremely sweet, and many Malaysians are extremely fond of the king of the fruits, the durian, a very thorny fruit. Most Occcidentals are put off by the pungent odor. This fruit is bought and eaten like crazy by Malaysians and people in the neighboring countries such as Singapore and Thailand. The thorny fruit has to be carefully pried open, and then the pulp, minus the seeds, is eaten. This fruit is actually a bane to diabetics. According to my niece, in spite of advice being given against excessive consumption of this fruit, many diabetics just ignore guidance, eat a lot of these, and come back with various complications, not excluding high blood sugar conditions.

I can personally relate to the consumption of this fruit and its effect on my sugar level when I went on a trip to Medan, Sumatra, in 1995. That year, after I resigned from the legal firm I was attached to, I—together with my good friend and colleague Lee Sik Kiong—decided to go on this trip.

One morning in Medan after walking around the shops, Lee Sik Kiong must have noticed that I was looking dazed and slow in my movement and responses. He realized that I was going into a hypoglycemic state. Sik Kiong is a great lover of durians. A stall was selling durian. I needed sugar, and this was a perfect remedy. He got the hawker to cut open the fruit, and both of us ate it. The moment the pulp got into my stomach, I could really feel everything becoming clear, and at last, I was my normal self again. For both of us, this was the first time we had tasted durian from Indonesia.

I have related this to specifically address the issue of diabetics eating this particular fruit. It contains a lot of calories. My advice is for diabetics to just eat one or maybe two pulps just to satisfy the craving.

Conclusion

It has been half a century plus six years since I was diagnosed with diabetes. Nature has been kind to me in the sense that, in spite of it afflicting me with this ailment, it has also ensured that I was given the proper mental strength, discipline, and proper environment, such as very good parental care, medical care, and good support, especially from my wife and siblings and many close friends and devotees of my guru who used to inquire and sometimes overdo their cares. However, I feel that they were naturally concerned about my condition after seeing me in the hypoglycemic state and hearing about my past episodes.

Even though I have related nearly all the episodes that occurred, I should reveal that it does not mean that these hypoglycemic attacks do not occur anymore. So long as I am a type 1 diabetic, I always have to be on the lookout for symptoms.

In fact, on June 20, 2013, when I tested the blood sugar level in the morning, the reading was about 2.4 mml (low). The instructions in the insulin pamphlet were to reduce the normal dose of thirty units Novo FlexPlen by two units—that is, twenty-eight units.

And this I did. I went for my usual morning walk. After about a half hour, my walking gait became unsteady. I stood still to do my usual test a few times. Things seemed normal. So I continued walking. After just about fifteen minutes later, I could see that I was walking very unsteadily. I stood still to check. Sure enough, the road and grass that surrounded me was sort of running away from me. Not wanting to take any more risks, I immediately took some glucose powder, which I always carried in my pocket, and with that, I also took some cordial drink I had with me. The effect was immediate. I checked again to see if my condition were all right and then completed the hourlong walk.

For the past two days (June 21 and June 22), after the alarm had gone off, I did not press the button. My wife had to get up, turn off the alarm, and check my sugar level. The average reading on both these days was 2.3 mml (very low). I was not even aware that she had given me glucose and cordial. So instead of getting up at four twenty, I got up at about five to do my ablutions and prayers.

Here, I have to confess that my wife was in a grumpy mood. Actually, the fault was mine. Being too careful, I did not take sufficient food. On the other hand, usually when there were symptoms of low sugar before I went off to sleep, I would either eat something or drink some cordial.

This happened on June 26, at about ten thirty, I could feel that I had symptoms of hypoglycemia. To clear my doubt, I did a blood sugar test. The reading was 2.9 mml (low). While sleeping, the insulin would further reduce the blood sugar level, and had I not eaten anything, I—or rather my wife—would have been put in very serious jeopardy. My physician, Dr. Thayaparan, advised me to keep the level at 10 mml at bedtime. I had asked him this before I went to India in 2010, and look at what happened at the ashram in India. When the reading was 2.9 mml, I took a piece of biscuit and some cordial. The next morning when I tested the blood sugar level, the reading was 4.8 mml.

Sometimes I do not even know that I am going into a hypo condition. In the many incidents I have mentioned, only those who are close to me or those who know my condition have forewarned me. All the falls and happenings that resulted were when I was alone. Or even if there were others, they were not aware of the hypoglycemic symptoms.

I have overcome so many obstacles and difficulties over the span related herein.These difficulties were more physical and mental and sometimes financial.Mental in the sense that I had to endure pain, long waits at the hospital in addition to the fact that transport in the early years was by bus.

However I am grateful to Nature for having given me all the support to carry on this diabetic life.

Fig. 1. Samuel Clinic

Fig. 2. Outpatient clinic then, now renovated and
known as District Health Office, Seremban

Fig. 3. Second-class ward then, now car park. 1) Single bedded rooms with revolving doors and 2) multi-bedded ward.

Fig. 4. Front view of old admission room, now converted and renovated into a drive-thru pharmacy. Background is the eight-story General Hospital, known as Tuanku Jaafar Hospital.

Fig. 5. Spirit lamp, the type used to test urine sugar and to boil water

Fig. 6. Type of needles and syringe (on right) used until the mid-1970s

1) Used since late 1970's

2) Pens from late 1980's

3) Novo mix

Flex pen used since 2012

Fig. 7. 1) Disposable syringes used since late 1970s, 2) pens from late 1980s, and 3) Novo FlexPen pen used since 2012

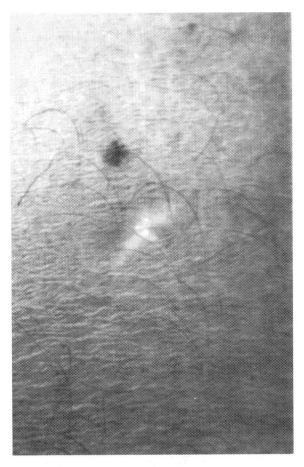

Fig. 8. Scar on left thigh

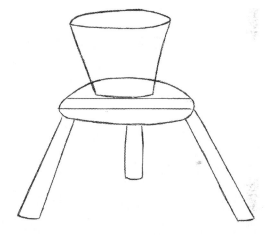

Fig. 9. Sketch of tripod stand, similar to one used then

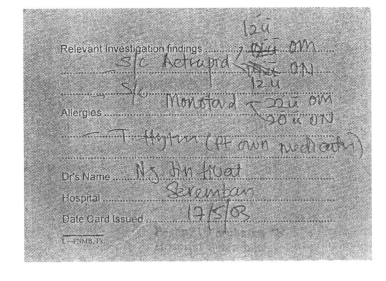

Fig. 10. Admission card

Fig. 11. Road leading to army camp

Fig. 12. Plastic sheet at scene of fall

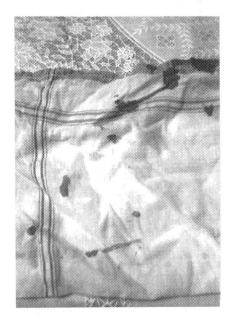

Fig. 13. Blood on handkerchief

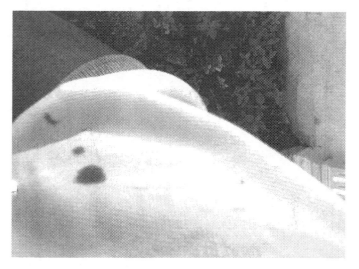

Fig. 14. Blood on T-shirt